More Praise for *Terms of Engagement*

"'Engagement' is to organizational performance what 'cloud computing' is to improved computational performance. Axelrod's model links the power of people in the pursuit of excellence. It is both an architecture and a process for responding quickly to changing business conditions."

—**Michael J. Freeman, Worldwide Training Manager, Agilent Technologies**

"By implementing Dick Axelrod's change principles and practices, our engineering team has a renewed vision for working together and a real hope for a brighter future. His engagement model is now a fundamental part of our people plan and the way we address significant change."

—**Hank Queen, Vice President, Engineering and Manufacturing, Boeing Commercial Airplanes**

"Dick Axelrod is one of our longest serving and most successful instructors. *Terms of Engagement* makes what he teaches in the classroom available to all. In an age when too many of us position technology and leaders at the center of our analysis, Axelrod does something profoundly important by redirecting our attention to the role of community and interaction in accomplishing change and achieving innovation."

—**Steve Laymon, PhD, Associate Dean for Business and Professional Programs, Graham School of General Studies, University of Chicago**

"I have seen these ideas in action. This is the fieldbook of change tools and techniques!"

—**Charlotte Roberts, coauthor of *The Fifth Discipline Fieldbook* and *The Dance of Change***

"Over the years, I've learned a great deal from Dick Axelrod about how to truly engage people in creating real organizational change. The learnings in this book are essential for us to understand in these times of relentless change."

—**Margaret J. Wheatley, author of *Leadership and The New Science* and *Turning to One Another***

"Dick Axelrod is among the best there is when it comes to bringing people together from across silos and hierarchies so they can make significant organizational contributions. If you want your business strategy to be more than words on paper, heed this book's lessons."

—**Peter Koestenbaum, author of *Leadership: The Inner Side of Greatness* and *The Philosophic Consultant***

"I experienced Dick's change process firsthand and saw amazing results! To attempt successful change without this book in hand is like entering a strange city without a GPS."

—**Sharon Jordan-Evans, coauthor of *Love 'Em or Lose 'Em***

"Axelrod provides the reader an opportunity to become an active participant in a different kind of change: the change that will energize an organization to new levels of performance and satisfaction."
—**Richard Teerlink, former Chairman, Harley-Davidson**

"If you are interested in change management, Dick Axelrod has written the book for you. The first edition contained a lot of good material, but this edition goes way beyond those ideas. I am going to use it with all of my organization design clients to ensure implementation."
—**Jay Galbraith, President, Galbraith Management Consultants Ltd.**

"My clients gobbled up the first edition of *Terms of Engagement*. Just wait until they get their hands on the second edition. Dick widened his own circle of involvement for this new edition through background interviews, correlations with the latest brain research, and new stories from healthcare, utilities, cities, and airlines—proof positive he is the real deal. This new change management stuff really works."
—**Christine Whitney Sanchez, President, Collaborative Wisdom & Strategy**

"In this new edition of what is already a classic, Dick Axelrod shares even more honest insights and actual examples. You will come away from reading this book with a greater confidence in the case for, and the how-to of, embracing the power of true engagement."
—**Amy Kates, coauthor of *Designing Dynamic Organizations***

"The first edition of *Terms of Engagement*'s pragmatic, principled ideas and methods ensured it would become a must-read classic for executives and change consultants alike. In the second edition, these ideas have been updated and additional materials added to each chapter to help people apply these now-proven principles and practices. And, of course, it is still a must-read classic."
—**Robert J. Marshak, Scholar in Residence, School of Public Affairs, American University, and author of *Covert Processes at Work***

"Engagement is the 'new organizational form' and key to the success of organizations and communities around the world. In describing engagement as a new model of change and as a way of working, Dick puts forth its principles and practices and tells us how to make it happen."
—**Diana Whitney, coauthor of *Appreciative Leadership* and *The Power of Appreciative Inquiry***

"I've experienced firsthand some of Dick's techniques for engaging people. Following his change principles has helped me tremendously. The first edition of *Terms of Engagement* is the most-worn volume on my book shelf; I'm sure the second edition will take over first place in no time. The new material on job design and brain science adds great insights."
—**Annette Freund, Vice President, Corporate HR and Support, Navistar, Inc.**

"What struck me when I read this book was the extraordinary combination—in one place—of pragmatic theory, real-life accounts, and practical advice for those wishing to implement major organizational change. Dick's well-researched, pragmatic principles provide solid foundations for engaging people to accomplish great things."

—**Tom Devane, author of** *Integrating Lean Six Sigma and High-Performance Organizations* **and coauthor of** *The Change Handbook*

"Terms of Engagement is an inspiring journey of engagement—combining a landscape of practice and principles, scientific insight, and compassionate wisdom. It will be an indispensable guide to anyone serious about improving the way we bring people together for noble and sustainable work."

—**Mila N. Baker, Senior Consultant, The World Bank Group**

"Terms of Engagement is all about the *why*, the *what*, and the *how* of employee engagement and makes the case better than anything else out there."

—**Matt Minihan, Partner, Sapience Organizational Consulting**

"This new edition of *Terms of Engagement* creates an even more compelling case for a new, different, and potentially more effective way to go about organizational change. If you're looking for current step-by-step help on change management, this is for you."

—**Sara Hakanson, Vice President of Organizational Development and HRD, Otto Bock Healthcare**

"This new version of *Terms of Engagement* is terrific. I love the distinction Dick makes between old change management practices and new. In keeping with this new thinking, he writes the book in a way so that you can lead change on your own."

—**Rick Maurer, author of** *Beyond the Wall of Resistance*

"This revision holds new and updated material that is essential to rectifying the current crisis of leadership and provides practical ways to assist changes in organizations that are not only needed but sustainable."

—**Angeles Arrien, cultural anthropologist and award-winning author of** *The Second Half of Life*

"Axelrod has been watching, studying, managing, and engaging in change for most of his life. Learn from this master."

—**Geoff Bellman, coauthor of** *Extraordinary Groups*

"In many corporations, people are fed up with change management. Dick shows how you can change organizations *with* people, not in spite of them. Use his insights and benefit from his practical experience. I promise you it will work because I experienced it myself."

—**Manfred Höefler, Managing Director, Integrated Consulting Group, Austria**

"The Axelrod team has succeeded in making a good product better. I confess that the phrase 'change management' leaves me cringing as only a good oxymoron can do—but all that aside, this book goes well beyond the superficial phrase down to the hardcore realities of organizations and how to make them fully functional. It is all about people, engaged people—and this book will get you there."

—Harrison Owen, author and creator of Open Space Technology

"In the search for simple ways to address the complex challenges facing organizations, Dick Axelrod provides welcome insights. The powerful principles and practices he names are key to change that works. The stories he tells bring the ideas to life. Bravo!"

—Peggy Holman, author of *Engaging Emergence* and *The Change Handbook*

"To say that the new and expanded version of Richard Axelrod's *Terms of Engagement* is important reading for managers and consultants is a significant understatement. It is required reading for anyone interested in and involved in organizational change. Richard Axelrod is acknowledged as one of our major contributors to the field of organization development. This work continues to reinforce his reputation."

—Peter Sorensen, PhD, Director of PhD/MOB Programs, Benedictine University

"We know a lot about engaging brains and brawn in the workplace, but we are just beginning to understand what it means to engage the whole person—brains, brawn, imagination, spirit, and common sense. Dick Axelrod's personal story and practical insights take us to a deeper place. Thank you for your tremendous contribution."

—Sandra Janoff, PhD, codirector, Future Search Network, and coauthor of *Future Search* and *Don't Just Do Something, Stand There!*

"Sometimes wisdom is made accessible to all. A great book for those serious about improving their organization, regardless of your definition of 'improvement.'"

—Barry Johnson, author of *Polarity Management*

"A timely and essential review for leaders wanting to enhance their capacity to motivate their workforces to achieve breakthrough business and organizational value."

—David Isaacs and Juanita Brown, cofounders, The World Café Community

"The new 'engagement paradigm' that Axelrod challenges us to embrace is effectively demonstrated in numerous real-life examples enhanced by guiding principles, graphics, and summaries at the end of each chapter. This is a 'must book' for anyone leading organizational change."

—Billie T. Alban and Barbara Benedict Bunker, coauthors of *Large Group Interventions* and *The Handbook of Large Group Interventions*

Terms of
Engagement

Terms of Engagement

NEW WAYS OF LEADING
AND CHANGING ORGANIZATIONS

Richard H. Axelrod

Berrett–Koehler Publishers, Inc.
San Francisco
a BK Business book

Berrett-Koehler Publishers, Inc.
235 Montgomery Street, Suite 650
San Francisco, CA 94104-2916
Tel: (415) 288-0260   Fax: (415) 362-2512   www.bkconnection.com

Ordering Information
Quantity sales. Special discounts are available on quantity purchases by corporations, associations, and others. For details, contact the "Special Sales Department" at the Berrett-Koehler address above.
Individual sales. Berrett-Koehler publications are available through most bookstores. They can also be ordered directly from Berrett-Koehler: Tel: (800) 929-2929; Fax: (802) 864-7626; www.bkconnection.com
Orders for college textbook/course adoption use. Please contact Berrett-Koehler: Tel: (800) 929-2929; Fax: (802) 864-7626.
Orders by U.S. trade bookstores and wholesalers. Please contact Ingram Publisher Services, Tel: (800) 509-4887; Fax: (800) 838-1149; E-mail: customer.service@ingrampublisherservices .com; or visit www.ingrampublisherservices.com/Ordering for details about electronic ordering.

Berrett-Koehler and the BK logo are registered trademarks of Berrett-Koehler Publishers, Inc.

Printed in the United States of America

Berrett-Koehler books are printed on long-lasting acid-free paper. When it is available, we choose paper that has been manufactured by environmentally responsible processes. These may include using trees grown in sustainable forests, incorporating recycled paper, minimizing chlorine in bleaching, or recycling the energy produced at the paper mill.

Library of Congress Cataloging-in-Publication Data
Axelrod, Richard H., 1943-
 Terms of engagement : new ways of leading and changing organizations / Richard H. Axelrod.
—Rev. and expanded ed.
     p. cm.
 Includes index.
 ISBN 978-1-60509-447-2 (pbk. : alk. paper)
1. Organizational change—Management. 2. Employee motivation. I. Title.
 HD58.8.A94 2010
 658.4'06—dc22   2010025145

SECOND EDITION
15 14 13 12 11 10   10 9 8 7 6 5 4 3 2 1

Cover design: Richard Adelson
Illustrations (except the Trust Triangle): Joe Lafferty and LifeTree
Interior design: Beverly Butterfield, Girl of the West Productions
Copyediting: PeopleSpeak
Indexing: Rachel Rice

To Emily,
elegant coconspirator in life and in work

The truth of what one says lies in what one does
Bernhard Schlink, The Reader

CONTENTS

FOREWORD

The Means of Engagement

We put great energy into trying to change our organizations, and it is always more difficult and takes longer than we imagined. Some of this is in the nature of change and the general human reluctance to give up a known though painful present for an unknown though possible future. Much of the resistance to change, however, grows out of the way we try to achieve it. Often I think that people are not so much resistant to change, which happens all the time, as we are resistant to imposition and to persuasive, new-age coercion.

The most common way we try to change organizations is through strong leadership, clear vision, enrollment, rewards, and training events designed to get the new message across. Leaders and their specialists huddle to devise strategies to get employees, customers, and the universal targets of change—the stakeholders—"on board." Those planning the change somehow think that it is they who are in the boat and others who are in the water. When people talk of the need for change, they are usually thinking that it is someone else who needs to change.

This mind-set is what drives modern change management methods that include many meetings, many presentations, endless discussions of burning platform issues, lots of process-improvement programs, and a basket of essentially leader-directed moves. And when the change process is too slow, the typical response is to redouble our efforts and drive faster. As if picking up speed will solve the problem of being on the wrong road. In some ways it may help, for we are able to get to the wrong destination faster.

The alternative to leader-driven change and leader-driven meetings held to drive the change is to explore the possibility of engagement, relationship, and democracy as the methodology that will get us to the right place. That is what this book is about—the tools and strategy of engagement, innovative ways to mobilize human energy in service of the institution or community.

The uniqueness of this book is its concreteness and its lovingly democratic values. It is very specific and creative about the choreography of how to bring people together, not to dance or to socialize, but to get something done. If you watched a change or learning effort take place, you would not observe minds whirling; what you would observe is people meeting with each other. We need a rational strategy, clear vision, and good information, which come into use when we talk about them. If you are interested, then, in how change and learning really take place, you end up designing meetings. Who should be in the room, how should we seat them and group them, what is the conversation people ought to be having?

The way we bring people together, then, becomes a major concern for how change happens. We live in a culture that believes that the way to plan a meeting to gain support for new ideas is to make a strong case, present it well, and ask for people's commitment. It is basically a selling strategy. If you look at the way we meet in organizations and communities across the country, you see a lot of presenters, a lot of podiums, and a lot of passive audiences. This reflects our naiveté in how to bring people together.

Also, when we do search for new ways to structure a gathering, we relegate the question to facilitators and process specialists. Too often we think it is a third party's job to worry about the people side of a gathering, it is the manager's job to give attention to what we want to present to each other. We act as if "process" and "content" are somehow separate questions and often at odds with each other. Even then, if you simply measure the amount of time devoted to content and process in each planning and strategy activity, "content" wins without a contest. A good group process is needed whenever two or two hundred people meet, and the tension between process and content is a fool's dilemma. There is no need to choose between the two—both are essential; they fail without each other.

The time is right for a book on how to bring people together in a way that defines a change strategy based on genuine participation and human interaction. And we need a book that is written not for specialists but for managers and staff people who need a good group process and yet do not think of it as their life work. How we come together, which is here labeled engagement, is everybody's task, every time we meet, and the conventional wisdom about how to manage a meeting is in serious need of updating.

Many of our conventional ideas about gatherings find root in the beliefs of one Henry Martyn Robert and his rules. Robert was a Civil War military engineer who grew frustrated with the lack of productivity he encountered in community work after the war, and he published a pamphlet about how to get things done in meetings. It went unnoticed until the turn of the century when a publishing house picked it up and it got wide distribution. Now *Robert's Rules of Order*, or its grandchildren, invade every conference room and meeting hall. There is no escape.

The contribution of *Robert's Rules* is the importance the book gives to the question of group process. The downside of the rules is the essentially legislative solution they offer to meetings and the way they promote the thinking that control and predictability are the keys to success. Even though, in most work settings, we do not follow the rules explicitly, the belief that meetings should be engineered for efficiency is still very much with us. We have this image that a good meeting is one where the presentation is clear and "PowerPointed," things move quickly, there is little conflict, and we don't waste time with feelings. This is the industrial model of relationships.

We need to amend this worship of efficiency. Workplaces and communities are human systems. Human systems require patience; they grow out of conflict and succeed when feelings are connected to purpose. Meetings have a deeper meaning than just to cover the content and decide something. Meetings are an important place where commitments and relationships are either chosen or denied. Every change effort holds a meeting at some early point to move the change forward, and it is often the experience we have in that meeting that influences whether we decide to commit to the change or simply give it lip service.

What is missing in the consciousness of many managers is the reality that the social structure of how we come together determines the real, human outcome of the event. You cannot have a high-control, leader-driven meeting to introduce a high-involvement, high-commitment change effort. High-control, efficient ways of coming together, symbolized by *Robert's Rules* and "good presentation skills," sacrifice the opportunity for relationships to be built both between employees and their leaders and among employees with themselves. If you want change to be supported, even embraced, you focus less on charisma, rewards, and motivators and more on honest conversation, high involvement, and strong, high-trust relationships.

A meeting also has a symbolic significance over and above the specific content it was called for. It is much like the meaning dinnertime has for our experience of the family (on those occasions when we eat together). It is when all of us are at the dinner table together that we get a sense of the whole. It is the moment we are physically reminded that we are a part of something larger. When we are on our own, we know intellectually we are a part of a larger something, but it is a thought, not an experience. At the dinner table, we get a concrete, visceral picture of what the place is like and how it is doing. Whether the meal becomes a warm conversation or a food fight, we still get the picture. The family dynamics and culture become visible at these moments. And if we no longer all come together for a meal, that too becomes a measure of our isolation and separate ways.

Same with an organization's culture. It becomes visible and is open to influence when groups of people are gathered in the same room. It doesn't matter whether we come together to get information, to learn something, or to try to decide something. The structure, aliveness, deadness, whisper, or shout of the meeting teaches and persuades us more about the culture of our workplace than all the speeches about core values and the new culture we are striving for.

This is why meetings are important. The experience of the meeting carries the message of the culture, and most critically, it is the quality of this experience that determines whether people leave the meeting with optimism and a genuine desire to make something happen. Even using the term "meeting" understates the importance of when and how we come together. What we call "meetings" are critical cultural passages that in each case create an opportunity for connection and the kind of engagement that this book is about.

It is right, then, to equate engagement with change. Each time we come together, whether it is a conference, a training session, a public hearing, or a large group meeting of employees, there is the opportunity to create a culture of openness, relationship, and trust in leadership. If these gatherings are done in a way that evokes people's optimism and trust in their environment, then whatever the content of the meeting, the participants will leave more committed and willing to invest than when they arrived.

If you are in the business of attempting to shift a culture or change the direction of the organization, then your methods of engagement will be the vehicle to make this happen. This is why this book is important.

This book, as a reflection of Dick and Emily's work over the last twenty years, offers the specifics of how engagement strategies can work. If we have held onto leader-driven and directive strategies too long because we do not know what the alternative is or how to implement it, then these questions are answered in the book. After you read this book, you will no longer have the excuse that we sustain leader-driven, directed change because we do not know what else to do. If you really believe that instead of engagement, stronger drivers are needed to reach your destination, then you had best not read the book. Better to be accused of innocence than negligence.

Regardless of your own philosophy of change, read the book and enjoy it. It is a much broader statement than simply how to bring people together. It positions engagement as a cornerstone to our future and gives every manager and staff person the skills and concepts that until now have resided primarily in the hands of facilitators and consultants. The bible can now be read by lay men and women, and in this intention, it is much needed and gently revolutionary.

PETER BLOCK

PREFACE

I was an eager fourteen-year-old when I started working part-time in my father's model airplane factory. My early excitement soon dissipated as I learned what assembly line work was all about. Putting balsa wood parts in boxes hour after hour is not exactly exciting work. I measured my time by the number of minutes until my next break. The time clock became my best friend. I punched in and punched out.

All of my colleagues had ideas about how to make work easier. For the most part, these ideas remained idle chatter on the line. Disengagement grew as the boxes went by one by one. With no outlet for our ideas, boredom set in as we watched the clock and waited for the buzzer to alert us that our next break had begun. Sure, I could lobby my dad over dinner or on the drive home, but that communication line was not available to everyone.

George, my supervisor, would often take me aside and give advice on how to get through to "the old man." George's advice was helpful at work and at home. Yet when I would offer ideas to George about how to improve productivity, despite my being the boss's son, the message was pretty much "Shut up and do what you are told." George was a good guy; he just believed that because he was the boss, he was right.

I graduated from line work to become a machinist's helper. There, I learned to put tools back in their exact place, not one centimeter to the right or left. I didn't know why Fred, the machinist, was so fussy. My job was to do whatever Fred told me to do. What I really wanted to do was learn how to work the lathe. Instead, day after day, I swept the floors clean, only to clean them over and over again. I learned disengagement firsthand.

LEARNING THE BUSINESS TAUGHT ME WHY ENGAGEMENT IS IMPORTANT

Work in my dad's factory had engaging moments as well. I had jobs where the clock was irrelevant. These jobs gave me responsibility. They challenged me to think. I ran the shipping department and learned the intricacies of working with truckers and shippers. I navigated a testy relationship with an alcoholic freight-elevator operator. I worked in the front office and learned the importance of cost accounting and inventory control. I worked on special projects to improve productivity and yield. Through these experiences, I learned that everyone has ideas about how to increase production while making work easier.

I was privy to my father's musings about how to motivate the workforce. Today, people would call him paternalistic in the most positive sense of the word. He really cared about the people who worked for him. He often stayed late into the night so that the machines would be in good working order the next day. He felt responsible and didn't want people who worked for him to lose a day's pay because the machinery didn't work. His efforts to engage people frequently did not bear fruit. Had *Terms of Engagement* been available to him, he would have devoured it. But it wasn't. He did the best he could, but unfortunately, it wasn't good enough. He was deeply hurt when the workers unionized.

MY FATHER INITIATED CHANGES WITH GOOD INTENTIONS—BUT THEY FAILED

He puzzled over why people didn't accept the changes he initiated. In his mind, his changes would benefit everyone. Seeing my father's name in graffiti on bathroom walls was hard to take. It made me realize something was wrong. I began to observe what worked and what did not. The vision behind this book began to take shape.

In college, not surprisingly, I studied industrial management as the heir apparent to the model airplane world. One day, in a class on time and motion studies, the professor droned on about motivation and incentive piece rates. He characterized human beings solely as economic commodities. I felt as if I were listening to someone from another planet. I recalled my working experiences. I knew his thinking was shallow and primitive. It was not in sync with the creativity and ingenuity I had encountered daily. At that moment, I knew there had to be a better way to motivate people, and I knew it was starting to take shape in my mind.

So I made it my job to study motivation at work in the military, as a young second lieutenant. I experienced one incident that taught me that leadership is more than giving orders. One morning during officer training, someone we did not respect was leading my squad and me. There was grumbling in the ranks as he strode toward us. When he shouted "Follow me," no one moved. We made a statement: we would not follow orders from someone we did not respect. I learned a powerful lesson:

officers had the power to give orders; soldiers could choose how to carry them out. (Does this sound similar to anyplace you've worked?)

When I left the military, I was fortunate to participate in early organization development experiments in the Bell telephone system. As the repair service manager for Chicago's southwest side, I led an organization that serviced about 180,000 people and Midway Airport. Team building helped my group become the top performer in the city in every productivity and customer service measure. I was especially proud of our safety record. Every day we put eighty-five trucks on the Chicago streets. We went an entire year without a traffic accident. We did not build that record by increasing the number of safety lectures or demonstrations. Instead, we changed the relationship between the supervisor and the crew.

At General Foods, I participated in early experiments in self-directed work teams. There I learned that when you increase autonomy, provide timely performance feedback, and offer the opportunity to learn and grow on the job, productivity climbs.

THEN I BECAME PART OF THE PROBLEM!

In 1981, the Axelrod Group began consulting to industry. Our primary method for bringing about organizational change in those days was what I now call "the old change management." You know how it works. Leadership hires a consultant and together they decide what is best for the organization. They then seek to create "buy-in" by selling the solution to the organization. We thought we made an improvement by adding steering teams and design teams to help with the work. In the end, however, it was still the same—the few deciding for the many. Change management needed changing.

In the late 1980s, we began to realize that something was terribly wrong. The change management practices we were using took too long and did not sufficiently engage the organization. Meaningful change did not occur. We tinkered with this method for a while, adjusting first one aspect and then another, but to no avail. The time was right for a totally new approach.

A NEW MODEL OF CHANGE CHANGED EVERYTHING

In 1991, we developed the Conference Model, a radically new approach to organizational change. The Conference Model engaged large numbers of people in the redesign of organizational structures and processes in a series of conferences (two- or three-day workshoplike events) and "walkthrus" (smaller sessions involving those not present at the conferences). The results were astounding. More people were engaged in the process. Accelerated implementation occurred. Organizations created a critical mass of people who cared about the outcomes. Capacity for future changes grew. Productivity and customer service levels rose.

We were not alone. Sandra Janoff and Marvin Weisbord were perfecting Future Search. Kathy Dannemiller was inventing Whole Scale Change. Harrison Owen was experimenting with Open Space, and Robert Jacobs was creating Real Time Strategic Change. Many others were experimenting with new ways of getting "the whole system in the room."

Our thinking has matured and developed since the early days of the Conference Model. In the beginning, we focused on getting the techniques right. Now our attention has shifted to the principles and practices behind not just the Conference Model but all large group processes.

We looked at our own work and the work of others and identified four principles we have in common. These methodologies all

- *Widen the circle of involvement* by including stakeholders from inside and outside the organization.
- *Connect people to each other* using a variety of dialogic methods and techniques.
- *Create communities for action* by creating forums for people to have a voice in change that impacts them.
- *Promote fairness* throughout the process.

Taken together, these principles and the leadership practices of honesty, transparency, and trust constitute what I am calling "the new change management"—a process that puts an end to the few deciding for the many; a process based on honesty, transparency, and trust. A proven process that creates increased employee engagement, which in turn increases customer service and productivity.

LIFE FORCED ME TO WALK MY TALK

In 1992, an event in my personal life reinforced everything I'd learned about change during the previous twenty-five years of consulting to businesses. I had emergency triple-bypass surgery and spent twenty days in the hospital because of surgical complications. Having your chest cracked open is a life-changing event, one I do not wish to repeat. As a result, I radically changed my lifestyle. I changed my diet. I added daily aerobic exercise and yoga to my life.

My engagement with this lifestyle change has ebbed and flowed. Sometimes, it feels effortless. Some days, I feel doubtful or even indifferent.

Nothing is more basic than changing the way you eat. Every meal becomes an exercise in decision making. Restaurant dining becomes an assertiveness test. What I have learned from this experience is that even when the stakes are high, even when one's very life is at stake, engagement does not come easily. Observing my own engagement with these lifestyle changes has given me new insights, patience, and understanding about what it takes for meaningful change to take root.

You can decide to change in an instant, but more is required in order for change to take root. I remember the instant I decided to change my lifestyle as l lay in a hospital bed, tubes running in and out of my body, my postsurgical scars on display for the world to see. Deciding to change is a necessary first step. But lasting change requires persistence. It also requires acknowledgment, feedback, and support from others. You can't get there alone.

NOW WE ALL HAVE A GREAT MODEL FOR CHANGE MANAGEMENT

In 2000, the first edition of *Terms of Engagement* hit the bookstores. People began applying the principles and practices. The most gratifying result of authoring published material is to hear how people with whom we never worked successfully applied the ideas we put in print. For example, I received a call from Billie Alban and Barbara Bunker, authors of *The Handbook of Larger Group Interventions*. They said, "Hey, Dick, did you know that American Airlines used your principles to transform the company? We're including the story in our book." Silence on my end of the phone. "No," I finally replied.

The American Airlines story, "Back from the Brink at American Airlines" (Bunker and Alban 2006, 86–96), cites the principles of *Terms of Engagement* as the basis for American Airlines' active engagement process. This process "fostered significant changes in involvement, transparency, understanding, and collaboration, which, combined with process improvements, saved AA 1.8 billion dollars" (ibid., 85). These savings helped American Airlines effectively overcome pervasive low-cost competition and the devastating aftereffects of September 11, 2001.

A LOOK BACK AND A LOOK FORWARD

First edition readers of *Terms of Engagement* were able to apply its lessons on their own. My hope is that you will do so as well. I have included a "Questions for Reflection" section at the end of each chapter to encourage you and support your learning. The most heartwarming outcome of writing a book is to know people have taken your ideas and applied them. I look forward to getting one of those calls that starts with "You don't know this, but . . . "

I'm very excited about this new edition of *Terms of Engagement*. In it, you will find the latest insights and practices for creating an engaged organization. It's been a labor of love and a joy to write. Talking with the dozens of people I interviewed as background for this edition was a graduate education in itself. By the time I was finished, I had more than four hundred pages of transcripts from which I extracted key engagement practices and stories to drive the lessons home. Welcome to the conversation—and to the possibility of a truly engaged group of people where you work.

Engagement Makes a Difference

W e're about to start a change process, and I think we're going about it the wrong way."

Hank Queen, soon to become vice president of engineering and product integrity for Boeing Commercial Engineering, and Charlie Bofferding, president of the Society of Professional Engineering Employees in Aerospace, were present for a talk I was giving about the four engagement principles that are core to *Terms of Engagement*. Boeing was just coming off of the largest white-collar strike in U.S. history, where more than fourteen thousand employees walked off the job, and Charlie had suggested that Hank come and hear what I had to say.

At the break, Hank pulled me aside, and with those words, "We're about to start a change process, and I think we're going about it the wrong way," launched a change process that ultimately affected the entire engineering organization. This process, based on the four principles that make up the new change management, resulted in a 40 percent improvement in employee satisfaction, along with many productivity improvements.

Three years later, the same employees who went on strike voted by a margin of more than 80 percent to renew their contract. Today, new programs, such as the 787 Dreamliner and Multi-Mission Maritime Aircraft, have added six thousand new jobs in Washington state. Production rates for commercial airplanes are increasing, and orders are up.

Every leader faces the eternal question, How do I engage people in the purpose of the enterprise? You might be like Hank, trying to rebuild a culture; or Carol Gray, trying to improve access to health care in Calgary, Alberta; or Jan Mears, trying to implement a global SAP process at Kraft Foods, Inc. *Terms of Engagement* provides the answer.

In my work with leaders in organizations large and small, I find them grappling with a turbulent environment where rapidly changing technology makes yesterday's innovative ideas obsolete. Reorganizations happen so fast, it is almost impossible to keep track of the entities' names. The job you had yesterday is not the job you have today, and it is not the job you will have tomorrow, if you have a job at all. Organizations find themselves existing simultaneously as competitors and partners. Leading in this world requires all of the physical and emotional resources leaders can muster.

Globalization requires organizations to find ways of working that span culture, time, and distance. All of this is taking place in a world where people have more access to information today than in the entire history of civilization, yet they are increasingly lonely, isolated, and disconnected. Extreme wealth and poverty live side by side, while the gap between them increases exponentially. Authoritarianism and violence are rising in a world where people say they want peace.

The changes are so profound and occurring so rapidly that drinking from a fire hose feels like a leisurely cup of tea. Yet this is our reality, and in this world, success belongs to organizations and leaders who respond effectively to this complex, chaotic environment.

HOW BIG A DIFFERENCE DOES ENGAGEMENT MAKE?

In the first edition, I responded to those who said the cost of engagement is too high by asking, "What is the cost of disengagement?" Now we know.

- Disengaged workers cost the economy more than $300 billion a year (Gallup 2010).
- McKinsey & Company, in a global study of successful organizational transformations, identified cocreation, collaboration, and employee engagement as key success indicators (McKinsey & Company 2010).
- Northwestern University found that organizations with engaged employees have customers who use their products more, and increased customer usage leads to higher levels of customer satisfaction (Cozzani and Oakley n.d.).
- ISR, a Chicago-based consulting firm that has one of the largest databases on employee engagement, discovered that engaged organizations are 52 percent more profitable than their disengaged counterparts (MacLeod and Clarke 2009).
- Hewitt Associates has an Employee Engagement and Best Employer Database of fifteen hundred companies. In companies with 60 to 70 percent engaged employees, average total shareholder's return (TSR) stood at 24.2 percent. In companies with only 49 to 60 percent engaged employees, TSR fell to 9.1 percent. Companies with engagement below 25 percent suffered negative TSR (Wellins, Bernthal, and Phelps 2005).

- A recent poll by Challenger, Gray & Christmas, Inc., found employee engagement to be a top priority for Chicago-based senior HR leaders (Challenger, Gray & Christmas, 2010).

THE OLD CHANGE MANAGEMENT

If you look at any major corporation or government entity worldwide, this is what you will see: leaders with an army of consultants creating new organizational directions—the few deciding for the many. Often, leaders and consultants try to soften the blow by creating steering teams and project teams. But most people end up feeling that their voices don't count. They are left on the outside, wondering what is going to happen. This approach to organizational change is so pervasive that few question it. It's just what you do.

Four beliefs are the hallmarks of the old change management: the few decide for the many; solutions first, people second; fear builds urgency; and inequality is the norm and life isn't fair. These beliefs are so ingrained that leaders and consultants do not consider their approach to change as "the old change management."

WHY DO CHANGE MANAGEMENT INITIATIVES FAIL?

Most change management initiatives, while professing the importance of people, forget real human beings are involved. When change management processes identify people as "change targets," they deny their humanness. Peter Koestenbaum, noted author and philosopher, says, "The essence of being human is the freedom to make choices; there is no escape" (P. Koestenbaum, pers. comm., October 27, 2009). Whether you are trying to create an engaged organization or engage people in the latest business imperative, leaders and those who work with them make choices.

Leaders make choices daily about the principles they follow, the methods they use to bring about change, and the ways they interact with others. Organizational members make choices about whether they will sit on their hands or engage with the organization's goals. These choices have consequences. Ultimately, they determine whether change will meet with foot-dragging resistance or wholehearted energy.

IS YOUR PLATFORM REALLY BURNING?

Popular theorists like Daryl Conner and John Kotter reinforce the notion of plug and play, order, and predictability. They aren't the only ones, just well-known theorists who reinforce the old change management.

Conner (1992) popularized the notion of burning platforms as a key ingredient for change: the way to get people to change is to light a fire under them. We'll see later how neuroscience research is showing how lighting fires may shut people down rather than start them up.

While not advocating burning platforms, Harvard professor John Kotter (1996) wants leaders to create guiding coalitions populated by senior management, which in turn produce strong visions for the organization to follow. These ideas represent the old change management—a series of leader-directed moves where the few decide for the many. In the old change management, leaders seek to create "buy-in" to a predetermined solution. Buy-in turns leaders into salespeople and employees into consumers, thereby creating engagement gaps that increase resistance instead of decreasing it.

Henry Mintzberg, the John Cleghorn Professor of Management Studies at McGill University in Montreal, writes in *Harvard Business Review*, "Kotter's approach sounds sensible enough and has probably worked. But how often and for how long? What happens when the driving leader leaves?" (Mintzberg 2009, 2). Mintzberg goes on to say that building community is key to successful organizational change, and I'll talk more about this in chapter 8.

THE NEW CHANGE MANAGEMENT

The new change management is a set of principles and practices that provide people with a voice in change that impacts them. Unfortunately, just as "Coke" is the universal word for soft drinks, "change management" has become the universal term used to describe all organizational change efforts.

Many believe the term "change management" is an oxymoron. I understand that you offend people when you think you can manage them into changing. I have chosen to fight this battle by offering a different way to approach change management. And instead of coining a brand-new term, I've chosen to put the word "new" in front of "change management" to symbolize the difference.

Every change process is different. Every organization is different. No matter how much planning you do, there will always be unintended consequences. After all, you are dealing with people, not machines. A principle-based approach to change is not only necessary, it's practical. The principles and practices of the new change management build a solid foundation for change, and they provide guidance when you don't know what to do.

Here are the new change management's principles and practices:

Principles

- Widen the circle of involvement
- Connect people to each other
- Create communities for action
- Promote fairness

Practices

- Honesty
- Transparency
- Trust

Taken together, these principles and practices create engaged organizations. In an engaged organization,

- People grasp the big picture, fully understanding the dangers and opportunities.
- There is urgency and energy as people align around a common purpose and create new directions.
- Accountability distributes throughout the organization as people come to understand the whole system.
- Collaboration across organizational boundaries increases as people connect to the issues and to each other.
- Broad participation quickly identifies performance gaps and their solutions, improving productivity and customer satisfaction.
- Creativity is sparked when people from all levels and functions, along with customers, suppliers, and important others, contribute their best ideas.

- Capacity for future changes increases as people develop the skills and processes to meet not just the current challenges but future challenges as well.

WHAT'S NEW IN THIS EDITION?

So what is new in this edition of *Terms of Engagement*?

- *Success stories—in the leaders' own voices.* First, you'll read new stories from leaders describing results from applying the new change management in organizations large and small. In the first edition, the stories and examples came from our own practice. In this edition, I've "widened the circle" by interviewing dozens of leaders outside of our own practice. You will learn from people like Gaetan Morency, Vice President of Global Citizenship at Cirque du Soleil, and Chris, a checkout clerk at Best Buy. You will learn the dramatic results they achieved and what it takes to successfully engage people in change. Most of all, you will learn the importance of honesty, transparency, and trust in today's world.

- *Setting conditions for successful change management.* Second, you will learn how everyday conversations and your regular staff meetings can become the fastest-track engagement opportunities there are. I'm using the phrase "everyday" in two different ways: in the sense that you can participate in these conversations daily and in the sense that they are easily accessible.

- *New phrasing for a tested concept: "promote fairness."* Third, I changed the title of the fourth principle from "embrace democratic principles" to "promote fairness." I did this with a lot of heartburn, but many people have confused the notion of embracing democracy with a political democracy. People from outside the United States often said, "While I support the ideas in this book, I could not talk about embracing democracy in my country as it would be seen as advancing the U.S. political agenda."

If you want to increase engagement, people must have a voice in issues that impact them; they must sense fairness in what goes on. Employees are often skeptical of leaders' motives, their own abilities to influence decisions, and the idea that they may actually have to take responsibility for outcomes. The true essence of "embracing democracy" is coming together to discuss issues where everyone has a voice, where information is transparent, and a sense of fairness exists.

- *Designing work with engagement built in.* Fourth, I've added a chapter on work design. It is possible to design work with engagement built in. Engagement increases when your work provides meaning, challenge, autonomy, and feedback. These proven design elements apply whether you are a janitor sweeping the floor, a researcher working in the lab, or the CEO.

- *Findings from neuroscience.* Fifth, you'll be introduced to the SCARF model and learn the neuroscience of engagement. You'll learn how the threat/reward response impacts engagement and how the new change management lights up the innovative, collaborative part of the brain.

- *Introductory illustrations.* Sixth, each chapter begins with an introductory illustration. This illustration provides easy access to the chapter's main ideas.

In every chapter, you will meet people and organizations who follow the four engagement principles and use the three engagement practices to create engaged organizations.

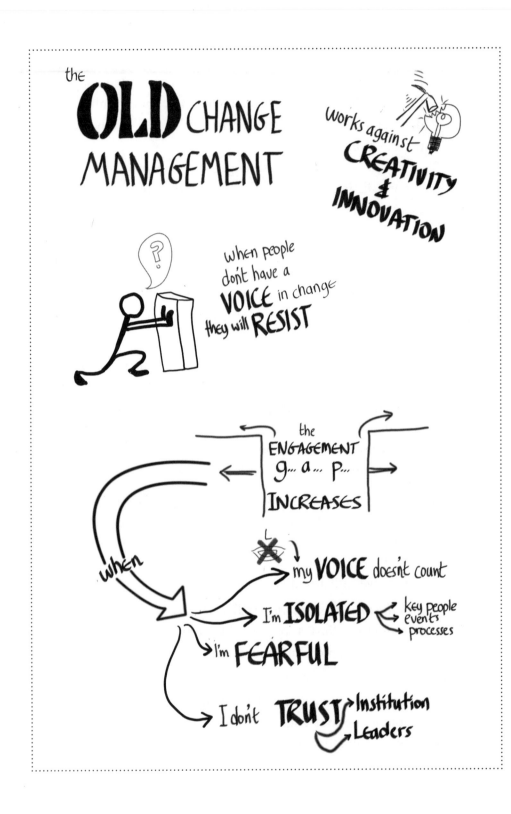

CHAPTER 1

Why Change Management Needs Changing

That didn't work. Let's do it again."

In organizations around the world, this is how change happens. You, the organization's leader, identify a problem and hire an expert consulting organization to create the solution. The consultants bring in their legions and you get your answer. Next, you try to sell the plan to the rest of the organization. But instead of excitement, you're met with indifference and resistance. Getting people on board becomes a full-time obsession. Your elegant solution, wrapped in a handsome binder, sits in silence on your bookshelf, an expensive reminder of what might have been.

"That *still* didn't work. Let's tweak the model."

This cycle has repeated often. To deal with the apathy and resistance that accompanies many change processes, consultants developed a change management structure to ensure buy-in. This structure consists of a sponsor group, a steering committee, and design teams representing a cross section of the organization. This streamlined organization strives to reduce the barriers to change that exist within the wider organization. But these groups and teams often fall into the same trap that exists when consultants work solely with leaders.

They go on to create the solution, and then, after making all of the key decisions, they seek to create buy-in from the rest of the organization.

Whether you are developing a strategic plan, improving a process, or redesigning an organization, the process is the same. This way of working is so ingrained that few question it.

THE DETROIT EDISON STORY, PART 1–WHAT NOT TO DO

For over a year, Detroit Edison managers had been working to improve their supply-chain process. They were following the acknowledged best change management practice, complete with a sponsoring group, a steering committee, and a set of commodity teams, along with an army of expert consultants from one of the big four consulting firms. Despite the hard work of many people from inside and outside the organization, they had little to show for it: lots of good ideas, none of them implemented. The lack of progress frustrated the sponsors, the steering committee, and the commodity teams—they just could not understand why they could not get the organization to support the changes they were proposing.

In spite of its critical importance to the organization, most people greeted the supply-chain improvement process with yawns. The only ones who seemed to care were members of the various committees—and even they were starting to show signs of disillusionment.

Fortunately, this story has a successful conclusion. The next installment—in chapter 2—describes how Detroit Edison abandoned the old change management approach to supply-chain improvement in favor of the new change management with dramatic results.

Four beliefs are at the core of the old change management:

- *The few decide for the many.* The change process works best when a select few—that is, leaders, consultants, and members of the sponsor team, steering committee, and design teams—decide what should be done. Populating these groups with the best and the brightest ensures success. This multi-level, cross-functional structure puts all key decision makers in the room. As a result, people within the organization will feel represented.

- *Solutions first, people second.* Because getting the right answer is crucial, developing the plan becomes everyone's focus. The groups work hard, often in isolation because they don't want to be distracted from the task at hand, to develop strategies, redesign organizations, and develop new cultures. While giving a nod to participation, they believe the best approach is to focus on the solution first and people second. The prudent course is to make the important decisions first and then move to widespread participation.

- *Fear builds urgency.* The best way to motivate people is to alarm them. A sense of urgency occurs when you light a fire under people, thereby creating a "burning platform." When people are concerned about their jobs or their future, they take action. Nothing of consequence ever happens without a burning platform.

- *Inequality is the norm and life isn't fair.* At an early age we learned life isn't fair and not to expect equity in our dealings with others. The title of Harold Kushner's book *When Bad Things Happen to Good People* says it all. Because life is capricious, we must constantly be on guard. It's a mean world out there; do not expect equity or to be treated fairly. As the saying goes, no good deed goes unpunished.

THE ENGAGEMENT GAP

These four beliefs combine to increase the engagement gap that naturally occurs in any change process. Any change initiative necessarily begins with a group of people who initially grasp the need for change. At this point, an engagement gap opens between those who want change to occur and the rest of the organization.

The old change management seeks to address this problem by creating sponsor groups, steering committees, and design teams. The problem is that as these groups immerse themselves in their work, the engagement gap widens between those who are part of the instigating groups and everyone else. Increasingly, these groups tend to objectify those not involved in the process as resisters and isolate themselves from the rest of the organization, fearing that time spent away from their work will cause delays.

As the engagement gap widens, resistance increases. This engagement gap, first identified by Peter Senge and others (1999), is an inescapable part of organizational change. No change effort can succeed for long in the face of an ever-widening engagement gap. Consequently, success depends on narrowing, rather than widening, the engagement gap. Why, under current change management practices, does the engagement gap widen?

Your Voice Doesn't Count

Whenever a change initiative is structured around a small group (representative or not) that designs and develops the overall change process, there is a risk of widening the engagement gap. The smaller the group and the less open the members are to soliciting input from the larger system, the greater the risk. When the gap widens, people come to believe that their voices do not count.

In such cases, people commonly resist plans in which they weren't included and, as a result, don't feel any real ownership. Or they have concerns about the decisions reached but feel blamed if they raise their concerns. Or they feel they have no choice but to accept the inevitable.

Excluded from the planning process, the "opportunity" occurs to decide how to implement plans. This typically does not feel like an opportunity at all but more like a manipulation. Is it any wonder that this process increases resistance rather than reduces it? When people are excluded from the planning process, the only opportunity they have is to implement the plans.

You Are Isolated from Key People, Events, and Processes

The old change management committee structure isolates leaders and organization members from one another, thus further increasing the engagement gap. The top of the organization has one view of the world, the middle levels another, and the lower levels a still different view. And customers, suppliers, and other stakeholders add another dimension. Instead of working together to bring their combined knowledge to bear on an issue, these groups work separately on their own discrete parts.

Here is a scenario I have witnessed repeatedly that demonstrates the problems of isolating leaders and organization members from each other. The design team works feverishly to develop a set of proposals. It then spends as much time preparing for their presentation to the steering committee as it did developing its proposals because the team knows how important it is to present the ideas well. At the steering committee

---

WHAT HAPPENS WHEN YOU
LEASH THE LEADERS?

Relegating leaders to the role of sponsors is a significant flaw. In this role, leaders are frequently isolated. This prevents them from contributing valuable knowledge, expertise, and insights to the design teams that make up the parallel organization. The only time they can contribute is when they review plans for approval.

---

meeting, the committee members put design team members on the hot seat. Soon everyone becomes defensive. Steering committee members, usually midlevel managers and union officials, feel that they are raising legitimate concerns based on their understanding of the organization.

On the other hand, design team members begin to believe that the steering committee has already determined the answer it wants. The design team goes back and tries to give the steering committee what it wants while staying true to its own beliefs. The steering committee waits for the next report, not quite understanding why the design team members are so defensive. After a number of iterations of this process, the steering committee arrives at a decision it can support. Then the process repeats itself when the steering committee members review the proposed changes with the sponsor group.

You Are Fearful, Withdraw, and Close Down

The inability to develop critical support for necessary changes results from the decision to use fear as a motivator. We have all

HOW TO STRUCTURE FAILURE
WITHIN AN HOUR: AN EXERCISE

Fear has roots in a lack of information. To demonstrate this, divide your participants into two teams. Call the first team the "planners," and call the second team the "doers." Charge the planners with developing a plan for how the doers are to put together a puzzle. (Choose a puzzle that can be put together in fifteen minutes.) Tell the doers that they will execute the plan.

Typically, the planners send the doers out into the hall while the planners develop their plan. While the doers are in the hall, the separation and lack of information produce negative feelings among the doers toward the planners. Some doer groups manage their fear by figuring out how to sabotage the work of the planners.

Once they develop their plan, the planners summon the doers and give them instructions. When the two groups operate in this fashion, they rarely complete the exercise within the prescribed one-hour time frame. But occasionally, the planners invite the doers into their deliberations and they develop and execute the plan together. When this occurs, the participants usually complete the task within fifteen minutes.

The old change management thinking is behind the scenes in the first method. It involves relatively few people in the development of the plan for change; then once important decision are made, it shifts its emphasis to implementation and buy-in only.

seen what occurs when widespread organizational fear takes over. People shut down. They stop working. Instead of focusing on improving the organization, they focus on self-preservation.

You Don't Trust the Institution and Its Leaders

When leaders believe inequality is the norm and life isn't fair, their actions often produce a lack of trust. Because people in

---

TELEPHONE COMPANY'S BREAKTHROUGH FAILS TO BREAK THROUGH: WHY?

Consider a telephone company's recent experience. The change management committees created a brilliant design for a new organization aligned with its customer base: they replaced the previous organizational silos with integrated business units. Both the sponsors and the committee members believed that they had created a breakthrough for this stodgy old organization.

Yet paralysis gripped the organization. Why? For more than a year, the design group had made decisions behind closed doors. Although the design group actively solicited opinions, not all departments and levels of people felt included in the process. When the time came to roll out the new organization, there had been so many rumors that people were negatively disposed toward it.

In the end, the design group could not bridge the gap to the new organization, with its greater responsiveness to customers and increased collaboration and teamwork. From the very beginning, people believed that fairness was absent. So they rejected ideas that would benefit them and the organization.

the organization come to believe that fairness is not present, they distrust leadership's motives, and any change process the leaders initiate is doomed before it starts.

A NEUROSCIENCE VIEW OF THE OLD CHANGE MANAGEMENT

Neuroscience helps explain how the old change management actually works against creative problem solving. Simply put, there are two human responses: we move away from threats and we move toward rewards. When the threat response in the brain kicks in, creativity and innovation decrease. When the reward response in the brain kicks in, creativity and innovation increase.

According to David Rock, author of *Your Brain at Work*, "Engagement is a strong reward state . . . Rewards activate the reward circuitry of the brain that increases dopamine levels in

TABLE 1.1

HOW THE OLD CHANGE MANAGEMENT PRODUCES ENGAGEMENT GAPS

Old change management beliefs . . .	produce engagement gaps
The few decide for the many.	Your voice doesn't count.
Solutions first, people second.	You are isolated from key people, events, and processes.
Fear builds urgency.	You are fearful, withdraw, and close down.
Inequality is the norm and life isn't fair.	You don't trust the institution and its leaders.

your pre-frontal cortex, decreases cortisone levels. It literally makes it easier to make connections, makes it easier to learn, makes you more optimistic, helps you see solutions, helps you find alternatives for action . . . So when you get an increase of dopamine in your pre-frontal region, you have essentially much better decision-making and problem solving, emotional regulation, collaboration, and learning" (D. Rock, pers. comm., December 22, 2009).

Rock (2009) has developed the SCARF (Status, Certainty, Autonomy, Relatedness, and Fairness) model to identify those factors that influence the reward response. When you apply the SCARF model to the old change management, it is easy to see how

- *Status* fades away when the few decide for the many. Status is about your relative importance to others. It's difficult to feel important when you know your voice doesn't count.

- *Certainty* diminishes when you are isolated from key people, events, and processes. You just don't know what is going on and you end up feeling more threatened.

- *Autonomy* shrinks when you don't feel you can influence your own situation. A feeling of helplessness sets in, fear takes over, and you withdraw and close down.

- *Relatedness* decreases as leaders and organizational members become isolated from each other at the very time you need connections between people.

- *Fairness* lessens when the change process appears to ignore evenhandedness. Self-interest takes over when you need people to look out for the good of the whole.

KEY POINTS

▷ The old change management works against innovation and creativity.

▷ When people do not have a voice in change that affects them, they will resist even if the change benefits them.

▷ Engagement gaps increase when

- You believe that your voice does not count.
- You are isolated from key people, events, and processes.
- You are fearful.
- You don't trust the institution and its leaders.

QUESTIONS FOR REFLECTION

▷ What are your own beliefs about organizational change?

▷ To what extent do a lack of voice, isolation, fear, and low trust exist in your organization? What are the causes?

▷ What are the upsides and downsides for you and your organization to continue using the old change management?

CHAPTER 2

Engagement Is the New Change Management

The old change management, with its committees, teams, and heavy consultant influence, contains the seeds of its own destruction. Remember part 1 of the Detroit Edison story in the first chapter? Here is how the organization dealt with the problems it was having with its supply-chain improvement process and avoided its own destruction.

DETROIT EDISON, PART 2

When Detroit Edison's leaders recognized that the process was in danger of collapsing, they decided that drastic action was required. They redesigned the supply-chain improvement process using the principles of the new change management.

Switching processes in midstream was not an easy task: the leaders did not want to throw out the good analytical work that had already been done, yet they needed to signal a shift in direction. The issues they faced were how to involve more people in the process so as to build greater commitment and how to build on the previous work while moving in a new direction.

Using the new change management, in a few short months they engaged over nine hundred people—one-third of the organization—in the supply-chain process in a series of large group sessions involving employees at all levels, customers, suppliers, contractors, and key union officials.

SIMPLE THREE-STEP TRANSITION TO THE NEW PROCESS

To avoid the "flavor of the month" problem that could have occurred from shifting the paradigms, the supply chain leadership developed a communication and education strategy to explain the change in direction, used the work to date on the supply-chain process as their starting point, carefully creating links from the previous work to the present work, and used current projects that required supply-chain emphasis when implementing the new process. This had the effect of grounding the supply-chain improvement process in real work, not imposing something extra on an overburdened organization.

What Success Looks Like at Detroit Edison

Today Detroit Edison has more than twenty-six active supply-chain improvement projects, with savings in the millions and growing. Engagement at all levels of the organization has replaced withdrawal and lack of interest. Furthermore, when the nuclear division needed to create a vision and strategy to meet the challenges of deregulation, it too used the new change management. Division management involved more than 650 people (more than half of the organization) in a three-day conference that set the direction for meeting the challenges of a new deregulated marketplace. At the same time, division management formed a critical mass of connected people who are committed to making that vision a reality.

THE NEW CHANGE MANAGEMENT IS MEANINGFUL ENGAGEMENT

Ask business leaders why their recent change effort did not live up to its promise. They invariably answer not that they got the strategy wrong but that they were unable to develop sufficient organizational support for the needed changes. Ask anyone who has participated on steering committees or design groups about their experience, and they will respond, "Wouldn't it be great if everyone could have the experience we had? Wouldn't it be great if everyone could have learned what we learned?"

Intuitively, everyone knows meaningful engagement is the key to successful change. If engagement is the new change management, then what does this mean for leaders?

It means you need to follow the principles and practices of the new change management. First, here are the principles. This list of principles is a process, not a menu. Applying each principle is vital.

- *Principle 1: Widen the circle of involvement.* Mere buy-in is no longer an acceptable goal. You must move toward deeply engaging people in the change process from the beginning, creating a critical mass of energetic participants who design and support the necessary changes. When you widen the circle of involvement, you go beyond the dozens who are typically involved in current change practices and instead involve hundreds, even thousands, of employees.

  In practical terms, widening the circle of involvement means expanding who gets to participate in a change process in two critical ways: including new and different voices and creating a critical mass for change so the few no longer decide for the many. Widening the circle of involvement also enhances innovation, adaptation, and learning (Axelrod and Cohen 2000).

- *Principle 2: Connect people to each other.* When people connect with each other and to powerful ideas, they generate creativity and action. Barriers to the flow of information and new ideas crumble as people forge links with others. Work also flows more smoothly because people learn how what they do fits into the larger whole and how they can access needed resources.

  When people connect with each other, they know each other. They stop being stereotypes, roles, functions, and members of that hated "other." They become human beings with their own real-life issues and concerns. People who are doing the best they can to get the job done, people with unique talents to share. They become people with mortgages and families who are trying to manage their lives. Connection begins with matching a name with a face, but it evolves to understanding who that person is, how he thinks, and what matters to him. Connection does not require sharing your deepest personal feelings; however, it does mean getting to know people beyond the facades of role and title.

- *Principle 3: Create communities for action.* No one can single-handedly manage today's challenges. We need a community of people who willingly apply their talents and insights to increasingly complex issues. Community is important because one person no longer has *the* answer; answers reside in all of us.

  When we create community, we move beyond a group of people who may have personal connections with each other. We create a group of connected people who have both the will and the willingness to work together to accomplish a goal that has meaning for them. Creating a sense of community in organizations is not easy because the requirements of formal bureaucratic structures run contrary to what it takes to build community. Nevertheless, we cannot ignore this task.

- *Principle 4: Promote fairness.* Fairness is a democratic ideal. Again, I'm not using the word "democratic" in the political sense; I'm talking about an egalitarian spirit.

  When this ideal is functioning, people deal with issues of self-interest versus the common good and minority opinion versus majority opinion in a way that ensures support and follow-through for the chosen course of action. Change grounded in these democratic ideals has the best chance for success.

  Fairness provides an ethical foundation for change. It produces trust and confidence in both the change process and those leading it. It is a universal principle that speaks to the human spirit, the desire to have a say, and the desire to shape one's own destiny.

Second, you need to apply the three key engagement practices of the new change management: honesty, transparency, and trust. These practices support the principles and build more trust. (I'll discuss these practices in more detail in chapter 4.)

HOW THE PRINCIPLES AND PRACTICES GENERATE ENGAGEMENT

These principles and practices help form the new change management. While building on the wisdom of the old change management, the new change management provides a framework for developing not only the support but also the enthusiastic engagement of the entire organization. Table 2.1 describes the underlying beliefs and results you can expect from the new change management.

TABLE 2.1

HOW THE NEW CHANGE MANAGEMENT PRODUCES ENGAGED ORGANIZATIONS

New change management beliefs . . .	produce engaged organizations
Widen the circle of involvement. Everyone's voice counts; the wisdom is in the room.	Creativity is sparked and accountability is distributed throughout the system.
Connect people to each other. Creating connections between people and necessary tasks produces better solutions.	People grasp the big picture and can identify performance gaps and solutions.
Create communities for action. Urgency is built through community. Everyone wants to make a difference.	Urgency, energy, and capacity for future changes exist.
Promote fairness. Fairness builds trust, which creates a foundation for collaboration.	Collaboration across organizational boundaries increases.

WHY THE NEW CHANGE MANAGEMENT WORKS

Just as the SCARF model presented in chapter 1 gave us insights as to why current change management practices actually work against innovation and creativity, it can reveal a lot about the new change management. Remember, the threat response reduces innovation and creativity, while the reward response increases these qualities. According to Rock, engagement is a strong reward state.

How does the new change management increase the reward state?

- *Status* increases when people are included in dealing with issues that are usually reserved for the organization's leaders. When you widen the circle of involvement to address critical business issues, everyone's status increases because people are now involved in discussions from which they were previously excluded. And since status is not a zero-sum game, it is a win-win situation for everyone.

- *Certainty* increases when people participate in what is happening. This is even truer in stressful situations. Although the outcomes may be unknown, being part of the process increases certainty. You don't need a set of MapQuest-like directions, but you do need a general sense of direction. According to Rock, "when you give people information, any information at all, you're decreasing uncertainty . . . you say there are twenty variables about this change and unequivocally we know nothing at all about nineteen of them, but we know this much about one of them. It doesn't make any logical sense that people would feel better. It's just that they've just gotten more information" (D. Rock, pers. comm., December 22, 2009).

- *Autonomy* increases when people believe they can impact their own situation. I have often heard, "I would rather be part of what is going on than have something done to me."

- *Relatedness* increases as people connect to each other and build communities for action.

- *Fairness* increases as people experience their voices making a difference, as they see themselves as part of a larger group of people who are doing what is right for the organization and its stakeholders.

Increasing any one of the elements of the SCARF model reduces the threat response while increasing the reward state, which means you increase the probability that innovation, collaboration, and creativity will be the hallmarks of your change process.

PREVENTING PATIENTS FROM BEING LOST IN THE TRANSITION: THE CALGARY HEALTH REGION STORY

Pat Gilroy is a patient in the Calgary Health Region system with spinal problems. Several years ago, her family doctor told her to make an appointment with a specialist or more damage to her spine would occur, but she couldn't get in to see a specialist. Not only couldn't she get in, she couldn't find out *when* she would get in. She called her family doctor and he didn't know either. While she waited, she worried that more damage was occurring. She, like many other patients in the Calgary Health Region, was lost in the system.

Today, Pat will see her specialist promptly. She can call her family doctor or specialist and he can tell her when her next appointment is. Wait times in the Calgary Health Region have been reduced between 10 and 40 percent, depending on the subspecialty. In the diabetes, hypertension, and cholesterol center, the wait time dropped from 96 days to 4 days (Bichel et al. 2009). Not only do Pat Gilroy and others like her know the status of their referrals, treatment will occur sooner even though the number of referrals in the system has increased.

In 2006, patients, doctors, nurses, and administrators agreed on one point: the referral process was broken. Everyone had his or her own pet solution for fixing it.

All of this changed when more than 250 patients, patients' family members, doctors, secretaries, decision makers, and others came together in two highly interactive conferences in Calgary to understand, identify, and resolve the problems of the medical access and referral system. During these conferences, Paige, a secretary in a family physician's office, said, "We need to know how the specialists want to receive the information." Brenda, a staff person in a specialist's office, explained that her office often received sketchy referral information. Dr. Nairne Scott-Douglas, a nephrologist, added that he often did not receive enough information to triage patients properly. And remember Pat? She explained that because of her long wait she had to go to the emergency room to get care—the most expensive option available.

Why a Few Smart People Can't Just Fix It

You might think that involving many people in the redesign of a system would lead to chaos and confusion. Why not just get a few smart people together and let them fix it? But the opposite happened when 250 people gathered to figure out how to provide better access to care. As doctors, nurses, staff, and patients and their families participated in "walking a patient" through the system, they learned that everyone contributed to the problem. In this activity, one person played the part of a patient, and the whole group learned firsthand about that patient's experiences as the person bounced around the system. Self-interest melted away as people learned that they were both the cause and the recipient of system disconnects. Soon, everyone realized that if the situation was going to change, the patient needed to be at the center of the system. Those 250 participants, instead of contributing to chaos and confusion, became advocates for change throughout the system, and no one had to sell them the reason for change.

What the Process Achieved

The conference process helped build a community of connected people who worked tirelessly to implement the new referral system. It began with our working with Calgary Health Region's leadership to identify a clear purpose and boundaries for the process. The purpose the leaders developed was to broadly engage people in the health system to collectively redesign the referral process between primary care physicians and medical specialists so that it supports communication and improves patient care. This became the North Star to guide people through the process, not allowing them to stray off course into other areas. We worked hand in hand with a design team that included doctors, nurses, staff, and patients to develop the various engagement activities, including discussions on how to recruit people to attend, the design of the conferences themselves, and the implementation process. Allison Bichel played a key role as consultant and project manager.

Today, doctors and staff are able to provide effective and timely care to more people like Pat Gilroy. This is important because long wait times to see specialists can have life-threatening consequences for patients with pressing medical issues.

DO TRY THIS AT HOME

If you try the new change management in your organization, you may see dramatic and innovative process improvements rapidly implemented that save time and money. You will also gain the most lasting benefit of all: improved relationships throughout the organization that will help you solve tomorrow's issues.

KEY POINTS

▷ The four engagement principles—widen the circle of involvement, connect people to each other, create communities for action, and promote fairness—provide direction for engaging your organization.

▷ The three key practices—honesty, transparency, and trust—are the basis of any successful change process.

▷ The new change management increases status, certainty, autonomy, relatedness, and fairness, which in turn lights up the creative parts of the brain.

QUESTIONS FOR REFLECTION

▷ What are the upsides and downsides for you and your organization to use the new change management as the basis for your next change initiative?

▷ How do the lessons from the Detroit Edison and Calgary Health Region stories apply to you and your organization today?

▷ How can you build status, certainty, autonomy, relatedness, and fairness into what you do?

▷ What will the new change management require of you as a leader?

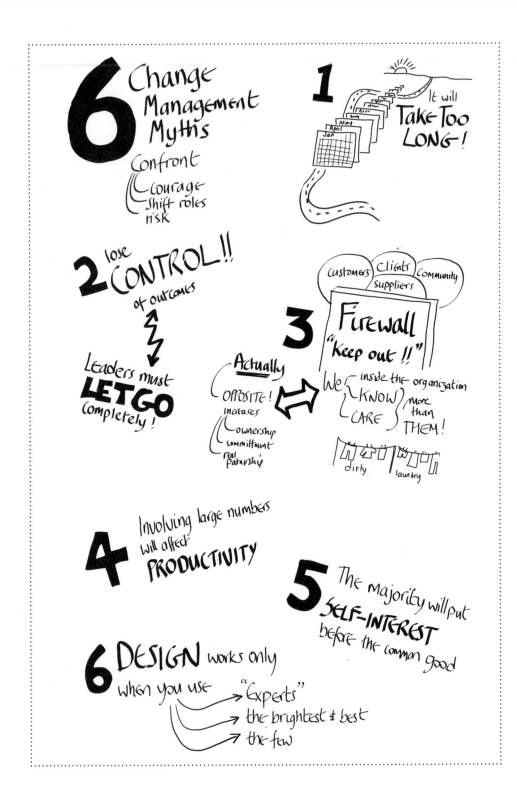

CHAPTER 3

Six Change Management Myths

When I discuss the new change management with potential users, they often raise a familiar set of objections, which I am calling "myths." These are the beliefs that keep leaders holding on to the old change management and prevent them from moving toward the new change management:

- It will take too long.

- Success requires leaders to completely let go.

- We must keep a firewall between the organization and its stakeholders.

- Productivity will suffer if I involve a lot of people.

- The majority put self-interest before the common good.

- Changes designed by the best and the brightest are cost-effective.

MYTH 1: IT WILL TAKE TOO LONG

Leaders look at the investment of time and money that goes with widening the circle of involvement and initially gasp. While the new change management does place a higher emphasis on including more people throughout the change process, the investment of time and energy pays dividends when it comes to execution. As you will see in the stories throughout this book, when people are involved in change from the very beginning, the time spent creating buy-in once the new direction is established virtually disappears and the change process proceeds with a life of its own.

MYTH 2: SUCCESS REQUIRES LEADERS TO COMPLETELY LET GO

As leaders contemplate widening the circle of involvement and promoting fairness, they sometimes believe that these principles will require them to completely abdicate their legitimate authority and responsibility, as well as the ability to provide input based on their knowledge and experience. Nothing could be further from the truth. The new change management does not mean excluding leaders, nor does it mean leaders must abdicate their responsibilities. In fact, their involvement is critical to success.

Paradoxically, as a result of the trust building that occurs throughout the process, leaders often find it easier to make authoritarian moves when necessary. So if you really want to be more authoritarian, the secret is to be more participative.

But the Leader's Role Does Change

What *does* shift is the essential role of leaders. Instead of being responsible for identifying both the problem and the solution, they are now responsible for identifying the issues and purposes, managing relationships across organizational boundaries, creating freedom within frameworks, and applying the principles of the new change management to engage others in the dialogue. Throughout the process, leaders focus on a variety of questions: What needs to change and why? What needs to be different in the organization as a result of our work? What are the boundary conditions? (That is, what is open for discussion and what is not?) Whose voice is required? Who else needs to be here? How do we build the necessary connection between people and ideas? How will we create a community of people who are ready and willing to act? How will we embrace fairness throughout the process? Leaders do not provide answers to these questions but ensure that answers are developed.

Oh, No—*They're* Going to Be in the Room?

Leaders are often concerned that if they fully and visibly participate in a change process, employees will not speak out or will blindly accept what the leaders have to say. Similarly, employees are often concerned that if leaders are in the room, they will not listen to employee concerns. These beliefs are genuine impediments. Leaders and employees must learn to work in an atmosphere where a give-and-take of ideas happens. Employees and leaders need to work together in addressing issues because each group has information the other does not have. Leaders have a view of what is happening in the outside world, and employees have information about what is going on each day within the organization. Both sets of information are necessary to address systemic issues. When leaders follow the principles of the new change management, they create situations where this kind of information sharing is possible.

MYTH 3: WE MUST KEEP A FIREWALL

Leaders who try to maintain a firewall between the organization and outside stakeholders, such as customers, suppliers, and community members, typically believe that others will not care about the organization as much as they do. This fallacy is used as a reason to omit customers, suppliers, or even people from other parts of the organization from the change process. Accompanying this myth is a fear that if we include outsiders in our change process, we will be airing our dirty laundry in public, thus alienating the very people who are necessary to our success.

Experience reveals that the opposite is true. Just as including those affected by a change builds ownership and commitment *within* an organization, it builds ownership and commitment with those *outside* the organization. As customers and suppliers work with you to build a future, they become invested in your success and become true partners in the change process, moving from making demands to offering ideas for mutual gain. It is not uncommon for customers and suppliers to offer ideas about how they could help reduce costs or improve the process as a result of their involvement.

For example, at a telephone company with which my colleagues and I worked, commercial directory-assistance users developed new procedures that benefited both them and the telephone company. In a hospital, doctors, nurses, administrative staff, and insurance companies worked together to improve patient care while reducing unnecessary costs. Many times outsiders who have been included in the change process ask to continue to be part of it due to their increased investment in the outcomes.

MYTH 4: PRODUCTIVITY WILL SUFFER IF I INVOLVE A LOT OF PEOPLE

When my colleagues and I first began to talk to leaders about the Conference Model, we would say that we wanted to take hundreds of people off-site for two or three days at a time and that we wanted to do this not just once but three or four times! We would look across the table and see people leaning back in their chairs as their eyes rolled. They were calculating the cost and wondering if it was worth it.

What we have seen repeatedly is that productivity does not suffer when more people are involved; in fact, many times it increases. We have seen telephone call-handling rates, manufacturing productivity, and customer service levels actually improve during conferences. It turns out that people understand the significance of involving more people in change processes, and those unable to attend the conferences put forth extra effort during these times as a way of supporting those who are attending the conferences.

MYTH 5: THE MAJORITY PUT SELF-INTEREST BEFORE THE COMMON GOOD

The fear accompanying the myth of self-interest is that the process will disintegrate. Some participants will try to improve their own departments rather than improve the whole organization. Similarly, individuals will protect themselves and not make decisions for the common good. Again, these beliefs are contrary to experience. For the most part, when people understand all of the issues and the role they and their departments play, they are willing to offer ideas and make decisions that benefit the whole. In fact, I have seen people offer suggestions and ideas that were not in their own self-interest at all because they were deeply involved in the process and understood the issues and opportunities. I have even seen people identify their own jobs as unnecessary! When people have the opportunity to be involved in making difficult decisions rather than having these decisions thrust upon them, the results are often surprising.

MYTH 6: CHANGES DESIGNED BY THE BEST AND BRIGHTEST ARE COST-EFFECTIVE

Certainly, widening the circle of involvement is costly both financially and emotionally. The whole change process instantly becomes more visible and the stakes become higher. But what is the cost of disengagement? What is the cost of brilliant strategies never implemented? What is the cost of change processes that increase cynicism and resistance and provide new material for *Dilbert* cartoons? What is the cost of talented people leaving organizations because they believe that their voices do not count? By contrast, throughout this book, you will read stories about organizations that have made the investment and see the benefits they received.

ENGAGEMENT IS NOT FOR THE TIMID

The new change management is not business as usual. It is not for the faint of heart and it is not for everyone. Applying the principles of the new change management is hard work that requires courage, risk taking, and perseverance. It requires meeting the six change management myths head-on. The reward is an organization that is flexible, energetic, innovative, connected, and responsive enough to meet the demands of a constantly changing business environment.

KEY POINTS

▷ Myths are just myths.

▷ Confronting myths leads to success.

▷ Leading the new change management requires a shift in roles.

▷ The new change management is not risk free.

QUESTIONS FOR REFLECTION

▷ Which of the six myths in this chapter do you believe the most?

▷ What would change if you no longer believed that myth?

▷ How are you prepared to shift your role?

▷ In adopting the new change management, what risks are you willing to take?

▷ What risks are you not willing to take?

CHAPTER 4

Lead with an Engagement Edge

In the North Sea, an oil platform caught fire and was burning fast. On it was a lone worker. He had a decision to make: stay and face certain death or jump and face probable death.

Leaders often call upon the burning platform when they want to create a sense of urgency. And while they might not know the original story behind the metaphor, the metaphors we use are important.

But beware of the burning platform.

WHAT HAPPENS WHEN YOU INVOKE THE BURNING PLATFORM

When managers invoke the burning platform, it sounds like this: "If we don't make this change, we will have to close our doors in six months" or "If we don't get the new product in three months, our competitors will eat our lunch" or "If you want to have a job, you'd better get on board." The hope here is that fear will create action.

To an extent, the strategy works because people want to survive. They will act when faced with a burning platform, but it is difficult to predict what choice they will make. Some will get on board, others will panic, and others will jump ship. Some will try to make themselves look good, others will try to make their coworkers look bad, and others will hide bad news.

When faced with a burning platform, people often choose self-preservation over the common good. And while choosing self-interest over the common good is a choice, it is a choice based on fear—not on honest dialogue or a trusting relationship.

Whether to join, engage, and put your heartfelt energy behind your work is a choice. People in organizations large and small make this choice every day: in their homes; at a local parent-teacher organization meeting; in churches, mosques, and synagogues; at Starbucks; and on a walk down the street. Everyone from the CEO to the janitor chooses whether to engage. To deny the fact that people choose to engage or disengage is to deny your own humanness and the humanness of those who work with you.

YOU NEED MORE THAN A GOOD SET OF PRINCIPLES

The four engagement principles (widen the circle of involvement, connect people to each other, create communities for action, and promote fairness) are necessary but not sufficient to create an engaged organization. The three leadership practices described in this chapter and the set of everyday conversations described in the next chapter form the foundation for the new change management, which ultimately leads to creating an engaged organization. The engagement principles, practices, and conversations shown in figure 4.1 determine people's decisions to either join you or stay on the sidelines.

FIGURE 4.1

THE NEW CHANGE MANAGEMENT TREE

THE CHOICE TO BE HONEST

If you've ever put together a budget, then you know how this game is played. You submit numbers that are more than what you need because you know your boss will cut them back. Your boss knows that the numbers she gets are overstated. So she cuts your budget, knowing she will not harm the organization by doing so. You put up a fight; your boss stays firm.

In the end, you both feel good. You get what you need and your boss maintains the organization's financial integrity. As a player in this game, you look out for what is best for you, not what is best for the organization.

While some might not view this as outright deception, the whole process requires shading the truth and expecting your boss to catch your deceptions.

How One Leader Ended the Game

Henri Lipmanowicz, former president of Merck's Intercontinental Region and Japan, put an end to the "budget game" in his organization by creating an honesty expectation: "The deal is, you don't play games with me; I don't play games with you. You submit the best budget that your team believes it can achieve and that's it. Done! I won't second-guess you and change it. Your budget is *your* budget and not one that I impose on you" (H. Lipmanowicz, pers. comm., September 2, 2009).

Henri's goal was to change the budgeting process. Traditionally, product managers would put together expense and sales forecasts for their products working separately so they could compete for the largest expense budget. Henri replaced this siloed approach with a process that instead invited the managers to discuss together how best to allocate resources across all products for a country in order to maximize income from all of them.

Transforming the budgeting process was not an easy task. At first, people did not believe Henri so they tested him. This required him to demonstrate that he could see through their ploys and that playing games with the budget would not work. Second, he developed budget planning software that made everyone's budget assumptions transparent. Every product manager could see the assumptions for other products in his country and also see the assumptions for his own product across all the countries of a region.

At the country level, the new budgeting software made it possible to instantaneously calculate the impact of changing the allocation of resources across products. Any change generated a range of potential budgets. At the regional level, for an area such as Latin America or Asia, the new software generated the same transparency, as well as a range of regional budgets reflecting various resource allocation options across countries. It was now possible for country managers and their regional vice presidents to decide *together* what would make the most sense for an entire region. When people realized that Henri was serious about ending the budget game and that transparent information was available, they gradually stopped playing the budget game.

Henri Committed *Himself* to Honesty

Henri describes the role of honesty in making the process work this way: "If you want people to submit honest budgets, you have to talk about it with them at length. Everybody from top to bottom hates the game. They see no way out. Breaking this cycle takes a commitment from many sides. At some point, you have to demonstrate this is going to be real. People aren't necessarily going to believe you. If you tell them, 'I'm not going to play with your budget,' you'd better not play with their budgets and be prepared to live with the consequences. You build credibility over time with each manager separately. People have to understand that they're not going to fool you. It's a no-win proposition to try to play games" (ibid.).

Henri even took this process one step further. When Merck's CEO asked him to generate extra income, Henri shared the current state of corporate finances with his team. He then asked what each of them could contribute to meet the new target. He did not allocate a portion of his target to each region, as is common practice. He just asked, "What can you do?" There never was a single instance when the sum of his team's voluntary contributions wasn't enough to meet his target. However, instead of the contributions from each region reflecting an arbitrary percentage, they reflected who was in the best position to contribute and what was in the best interests of the whole division.

It took a while for Henri to end the game playing. When he did, he also ended the need for long, drawn-out budgeting meetings where everyone knows the game and how the game ends; staffs pad their budgets in anticipation of several budgeting rounds because in the end the boss increases the sales target and cuts the expenses.

The trusting atmosphere Henri created made people feel safe enough to submit budgets much more ambitious than they would have dared under the old system. Exceptional results followed—results impossible to achieve under the old system.

Reorganizations, budgeting conversations, and times of economic distress are often fraught with disengagement. Yet in Merck's example, we see how the choice to be honest is crucial to engaging people in the most difficult tasks.

THE CHOICE TO BE TRANSPARENT

Transparency is the free flow of clear information. As the following story shows, you can use a variety of methods to ensure that transparency permeates your organization.

TRANSPARENCY AT THE AMERICAN SOCIETY OF QUALITY

Paul Borawski is the executive director and chief strategic officer for the American Society of Quality (ASQ), the world's leading authority on quality for more than sixty years. ASQ has been the sole administrator of the prestigious Malcolm Baldrige National Quality Award since 1991. This 93,000-member organization spans the globe with members in 140 countries and offices in China, India, Mexico, and the United States. ASQ has a couple hundred paid staff and four thousand dedicated member leaders. Member leaders are volunteers who help with the work of the society.

One of the tricky parts of association leadership is working with both paid staff and volunteers. Volunteers are the lifeblood of an association. If you waste volunteers' time, if they feel that they don't count, they leave. This fact is not lost on Paul. In fact, he carries this mind-set over to the way he works with paid staff. He believes you are foolish if you don't recognize that paid staff may not leave in body, but they may leave in spirit. Paul believes "bringing your best to the table is a choice whether staff or volunteer" (P. Borawski, pers. comm., September 5, 2009).

Core to Paul's approach is transparency. Paul puts it this way: "I've always believed that organizations that think they are hiding information are kidding themselves" (ibid.). At ASQ, only two types of information are not available to everyone: personal performance data and personal salary information. Everything else is transparent.

If you walk the halls at ASQ, you will see a lot of performance data and financial reports. You won't see any tax statements, although they are posted on the Web site. Executives spend two days each quarter in business plan reviews that include financial performance and a lot more. Then all staff are invited to quarterly business plan update sessions. Everyone is welcome to attend, learn, and ask questions. Every Friday at lunch, one of the six executives meets with staff in the cafeteria. At these meetings people ask questions like, "Can you explain what you did with this paid time off practice?" or, "Why did the board do this?" The role of the executive in these sessions is to listen and provide factual, transparent responses.

Transparency does not end with the paid staff. Remember those four thousand member leaders? They participate in "ideas to action" sessions. These events, sometimes several days long, provide an opportunity to share ideas and get feedback on the organization's vision and strategy, performance indicators, and other issues. These are working sessions where participants develop recommendations and plans to respond to current issues facing the organization.

Transparency is present when ASQ makes tough decisions. When reductions in staff were in order, the staff received information about not just the reductions but the logic behind the decision. This made the decision, the information used to make the decision, and the thought process behind the decision transparent. ASQ's goal was to handle the reductions in force mostly through attrition. Every quarter people received information about eliminated jobs and progress toward the staffing goal. In the end, not all the reductions occurred through attrition. But again, transparency ruled the day. Information about how ASQ would treat those who lost their jobs was available for all to see. Because the process was transparent, people could make their own decisions about its efficacy.

Is transparency worth it? Paul Borawski thinks it is. Here's how ASQ used to do strategic planning. Paul had a strategic planning committee, and every couple of years the members would meet privately to update the strategic plan. They would then take the plan to the board, which would approve the plan.

Who owned the plan? Who really understood the plan? Not the board and certainly not the organization. "You pay the price over and over again when things aren't transparent" (ibid.). No one really understands the plan or the thinking behind it, so when you try to implement the plan, you are always backtracking. When transparency is not present, people don't understand the rationale behind what you are doing. Initiatives slow down and they move in the wrong direction.

When transparency is present, you've got hundreds of people who understand the thinking behind the plan, and when they get questions from their peers, they can say, "I support this; here is why." As a leader, you are no longer feeling the burden that comes with being the sole champion; you have hundreds of champions working alongside you.

THE CHOICE TO BUILD TRUST

Trust is not an accident. We choose behaviors that make us trustworthy. We choose behaviors that indicate our trust in others.

Engaged at Best Buy

"I love this place," the cashier said.

"Why is that?" I replied.

"Because they trust me to make the right decisions. I've worked other places and there is always someone looking over your shoulder. Not here. They trust me to do the right thing."

I was at Best Buy purchasing a jump drive. Because the store did not seem to be very busy, I asked Chris, who was working checkout, what was it like to work there. I had just read an article describing Best Buy's emphasis on employee engagement. So I decided to take an unscientific random sample while waiting in the checkout line. Chris's answer mirrored everything I experienced in the store.

Wouldn't you like to have people say "I love this place" in your organization? Loving a workplace goes way beyond making people feel happy. Chris's love for Best Buy is born from management's trust that she will make the right decisions. For Best Buy, having employees who love to work there has bottom-line implications. Best Buy estimates that a 2 percent increase in employee engagement at one of its electronics stores corresponds, on average, to a $100,000 annual rise in sales at that location (Conlin 2009).

Engaged at Allstate

Carla Zuniga is vice president of operations for Allstate Insurance Company. Between 2007 and 2009, her organization saved $60 million while improving the customers' experience. Allstate is like many big organizations where people are skeptical of change and treat new initiatives as the latest "flavor of the month." So when Carla and her leadership team introduced a transformation process that sought to include nearly all of Operation's forty-five hundred employees, you can imagine the skepticism.

They had a lot of what Carla calls "baggage" to overcome. In some cases, employees were not familiar with the leaders; in other cases, employees knew the leaders but did not trust them based on past experiences. And almost everyone believed that all of this inclusiveness would probably go away after a while. Sound familiar?

Carla describes her early efforts this way: "Initially it was about dialogue, getting any level of leader, especially myself and my boss, out into the organization having every kind of conversation possible. That meant big meetings, tiny meetings, meet-and-greet sessions, one-on-ones—it didn't matter what level it was. You did whatever you needed to do to reinforce that you, the leader, were very committed, and the more they shared, the better you would be as a leader because you had a much broader point of view" (C. Zuniga, pers. comm., August 4, 2009).

Making commitments and keeping one's word were essential for building trust. But beyond that, Carla removed leaders whose behaviors kept getting in the way.

WHY HONESTY, TRANSPARENCY, AND TRUST ARE IMPORTANT

Tony Simons is the author of *The Integrity Dividend: Leading by the Power of Your Word* and associate professor of management and organization behavior at Cornell's School of Hotel Administration. He defines integrity simply: integrity is keeping your word or, in the vernacular, walking your talk. In his research, he has identified a causal chain regarding integrity. Simons describes the chain: "Where employees feel their managers keep promises and live by the values they describe, they trust their managers more" (Simons 2008, 11).

"So it was right that our leaders felt pressure to live up to their word, to be honest, to be transparent, and to be trustworthy. In doing so, they received a double bonus. First, they received a bonus for subscribing to these values because people like to work for organizations and people whose values they admire. Second, they received a bonus when they behaved in a way consistent with their values" (Ibid., 11).

What does this bonus look like? Simons explains, "Where employees trust their managers more, they become more emotionally committed to the company, caring more deeply about its mission and taking pride in working for it. In short, high integrity among managers leads to lower employee turnover and superior customer service, all leading to high profitability" (ibid., 11). In fact, Tony found that an increase of one-eighth of a point on his integrity survey correlated to a 2.5 percent increase in revenues. The choice to be honest, transparent, and trustworthy, and then to live by the values you subscribe to, pays big dividends in customer service and profitability.

KEY POINTS

▷ Everyone makes the choice about whether or not to engage.

▷ Trust involves choices.

▷ The honesty expectation creates safety.

▷ Transparency provides the information necessary for people to make choices.

▷ Trust builds through multiple conversations.

▷ Integrity, the power of keeping your word, has bottom-line implications.

QUESTIONS FOR REFLECTION

▷ Think of a current situation where you would like to engage others. What is your goal? What would you like to be different?

▷ What kind of relationship do you currently have with people you would like to engage? What kind of relationship do you want to have?

▷ What will you need to stop, start, or continue to do to engage people using the concepts identified in this chapter?

▷ What will success require of you?

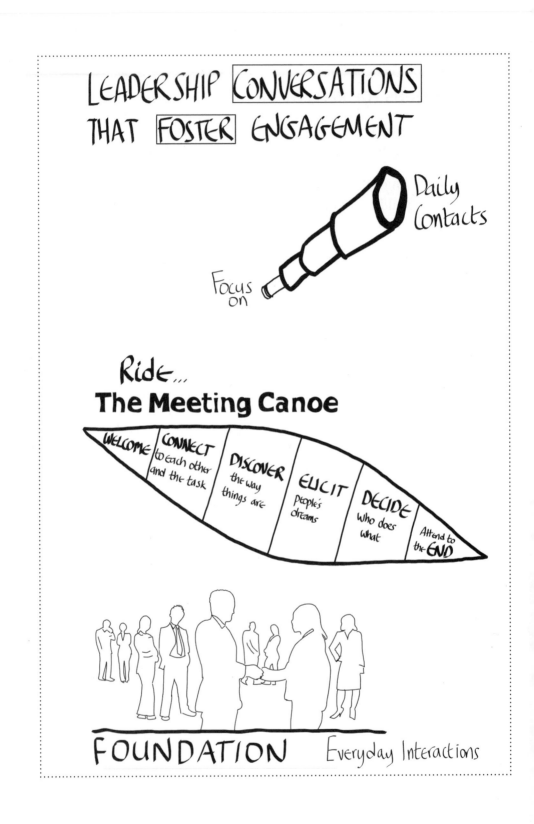

CHAPTER 5

Leadership Conversations That Foster Engagement

In this chapter, we will explore leadership conversations that support the new change management's principles and practices. These conversations, when done well, help form the basis for change. In these conversations, relationships grow as trust builds.

The leaders of a division of a global high-tech organization were poring over the results of their latest engagement survey. One number popped out at them: their dismal scores in employee recognition. They had to do something. So, being good leaders, they took charge and went about fixing the problem. They met frequently to discuss what they should do. After several meetings, the leaders decided the answer was to institute a recognition program. The program was complete with sweatshirts, coffee mugs, and the usual trinkets with the company logo. You know—the ornaments that end up as clutter on your desk.

A year later, when the leaders received the newest scores, they went immediately to the recognition section. They were sure that this year's scores would reflect their hard work. But to their surprise, nothing had changed. Recognition was still dismal. They couldn't believe it. What did these people want?

What would it take to satisfy them? Didn't they realize the time, effort, and money that went into the recognition program, especially during tough times?

With the best of intentions, the leaders acknowledged the problem with their recognition scores and set out to do something. After all, if the scores were low, then they as leaders were at fault, and it was their job to solve the problem. If you are a responsible leader that is what you do; when there is a problem, you solve it—especially when you think your own behavior might be the cause.

But while the leaders devised a "solution," they missed an important point in any survey process. They forgot to include the people who completed the survey in discussing the data and deciding what to do about it. What they failed to realize was that, while the survey indicated a problem, it could not tell them why people had responded the way they did. The survey worked much like a thermometer: it revealed the temperature but not the underlying cause. To learn why the scores were low, the leaders needed to discuss the results with the people who had the answers: the employees in the organization.

Had they asked, they would have learned that the recognition people wanted was an appreciation of the long hours they worked, an understanding of the stress caused by computer systems that periodically crashed and resulted in their losing hours of work, and an acknowledgment of their dedication to getting the job done despite the obstacles. Had leadership walked around and listened to people, helping them remove the roadblocks they faced and just saying "Thank you," the result might have been very different. In the words of one employee, "The last thing we needed was another pizza thrown at us."

STOP THROWING PIZZAS AT PROBLEMS

Creating an engaged organization means you sweat the small stuff—you focus on daily contacts. Why? Because the basis for an engaged organization is conversations that take place in the halls, beside desks, and as you do your work. These day-to-day contacts are where people decide how much effort they will put behind the organization's goals.

In case you are wondering why this is important, consider the following: "A review of the [workplace] climate survey literature reveals a very interesting generalization. It does not matter when the study is done . . . it does not matter where the study is done . . . and it does not matter what occupational group is studied . . . The results are always the same. About 75 percent of the workforce surveyed will say that the worst single aspect of their job, the most stressful aspect of their job, is their immediate supervisor" (Hogan 2007, 106).

Daily contacts can create a workplace where doing the simplest task is a hassle or a workplace where people thrive. If you want to create the second type of workplace, then you must hold four leadership conversations. It is in these conversations where people decide whether you care about them or not. It is here where they decide if you are trustworthy. It is in these conversations where people decide how they will treat your next idea and whether to join in or sit on their hands. The four conversations are not sexy and they are not gimmicks, but when you apply them with a sincere intention to help people in your organization thrive, they work.

Here are the four leadership conversations that, when supported by honesty, transparency, and trust, help form the foundation for applying the principles of the new change management.

EVERYDAY LEADERSHIP CONVERSATION 1: FIND OUT WHAT IS IMPORTANT TO THE OTHER PERSON

In workshops, I ask participants to discuss with the person sitting next to them the following question for four minutes: What do you care about at work and why? When the four minutes are up, people do not want to disengage from the conversation because they find it so interesting.

What happens during these conversations? First, people discover what they have in common. They learn they care about similar matters. Second, the act of listening strengthens their relationship. This makes it easier for them to take action on issues each of them finds important.

If you don't believe me, try this: ask someone at work what is important to him or her and just listen. You'll be surprised. If you're thinking you don't have time to do this, remember that it takes only four minutes.

What can happen when you dare to listen? At a global manufacturing company, a business unit leadership team conducted interviews with the employees. During the interviews, the leaders asked, "What do you care about at work and why?" At the top of the list was the ability to learn, grow, and develop on the job. Months later, when the leadership team announced the organization's goals for the year, the employees were astounded. Right near the top, next to cost reduction, sales, and profit goals, were goals focused on supporting employees' desire to learn, grow, and develop on the job. What impact do you think this had on morale and productivity? This business unit went on to be one of the organization's most productive business units that year.

EVERYDAY LEADERSHIP CONVERSATION 2:
SUPPORT OTHERS IN ACHIEVING THEIR GOALS

You can find many ways to support people in achieving their goals. It all starts when you ask others what kind of support they need. Listen carefully and you'll know what to do.

Support comes in many forms:

- Provide people with time and money to do their work.
- Make others available so they can help out.
- Answer important questions.
- Help people navigate bureaucracy.
- Provide the necessary training.
- Make sure people have the proper systems and tools to do their work.
- Acknowledge them with thanks and pats on the back.

Put the same amount of time and energy behind helping others achieve what they find important as you would put into doing something that you care about. If you treat employees' goals as if they were your own, you will find that when you ask your employees to support your goals, they will be more likely to join in. In many cases, supporting what they want will help you achieve what you want.

When I was a young manager, my boss, Ed Torongo, brought me into his office and said, "Now that I've hired you, my job is to make sure you are successful." You can imagine my shock and surprise. No one had ever said that to me before. What I had always heard from bosses was criticism. Ed provided me with all of the encouragement, training, and resources I needed to be successful. He didn't hold back when it came to criticism, but I always knew he was in my corner. The result was that I performed better in that job than in any of my previous work assignments.

EVERYDAY LEADERSHIP CONVERSATION 3: SHARE WHAT YOU CARE ABOUT

Stop telling people why they should change. Start talking about what is important to you. Be honest; speak from your heart.

What can happen when you share what you care about? In one case, recovering alcoholics, doctors, and nurses were talking about how to improve treatment services. The conversation began with the usual ideas: making the community a better place and helping people. The conversation was flat. Eyes began to glaze over. Everyone had had this conversation before. Then one person got up and told his story, how when he was in need, people listened to him. They answered his plea for help. They got him into treatment. They cared about him when there wasn't much to care about. His goal was simple; he wanted to give back to the community, to care for others in the way people cared for him.

Howard Gardner says, "The most important ingredient for a story to embody is truth, and the most important trait for a leader to have is integrity" (Gardner 2006, 112). No matter how compelling the facts, how dramatic or memorable the presentation, the most important trait a leader needs is honesty.

Honesty begins when you move from telling people why something is good for them to why it is important to you. Here's a simple question: If you are not willing to talk about what you care about, if you are not willing to tell the truth, then why should anyone else care?

EVERYDAY LEADERSHIP CONVERSATION 4: PAY ATTENTION TO MEETINGS

Meetings are the most overlooked fast-track engagement opportunity available. Every boring, time-wasting, energy-draining meeting you attend saps energy from the system. The fastest, easiest way to engage your organization is to pay attention to your meetings.

Because meetings are engagement opportunities, look beyond the typical notions of what makes for a good meeting. It's not that agendas and efficient meeting structures aren't important. It's just that they aren't enough. Meetings need to be more than something people endure; meetings need to create energy to take action on important issues.

TAKE A RIDE IN THE MEETING CANOE

The canoe-shaped blueprint in figure 5.1 helps us create meetings with an engagement framework. The shape of the canoe represents a conversation that starts out small, gets bigger as the group discovers the way things are and elicits people's dreams, and narrows as decisions emerge. The "meeting canoe" is the boat in which we travel, where everyone's contributions are oars that pull us to our final destination.

The meeting canoe works for two-person conversations and for groups of two hundred. Our son, David, was a professional ski instructor at Breckenridge, Colorado. One day he decided to use the meeting canoe framework when working with his clients. He would start by making his clients feel welcome, discover the current state of their skills, talk to them about their hopes for the lesson, develop a lesson plan, and attend to the end by debriefing the lesson with them. As soon as David started using the meeting canoe, his "request rate" went up, something very important to a ski instructor. As a result, David began to share the meeting canoe with his ski instructor buddies. And guess what? Their request rates went up. In chapter 8, we'll describe how Allstate used the meeting canoe to design large group sessions to redesign parts of the organization.

First, let's review the elements of the meeting canoe.

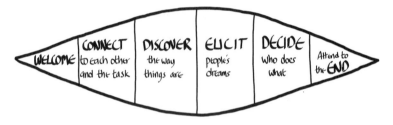

FIGURE 5.1

THE MEETING CANOE

Start by Making People Feel Welcome

Your welcome can be as simple as a handshake or as elaborate as having a string quartet create a mood of harmony and peace. Whatever welcome you plan, it should make people feel special as soon as they arrive.

Pay attention to the room. The room sets the stage and influences what happens. Try to work in a room with natural light and plenty of wall space. Make sure everyone can see and hear what's going on without straining.

Pay attention to the seating. In one organization we know, every meeting room had a T-shaped seating arrangement. In the center of the room was a long row of tables, and at the head, forming the T, was a table for the LCD projector. In addition, chairs were lined up against the wall, so it was clear that some people had seats at the table and some didn't. Contrast this with an organization that furnished every meeting room with round tables. Which meeting would you want to attend?

Find Ways to Create Connections Among People and to the Meeting's Purpose

In most organizations today, people go from meeting to meeting without taking a pause to know which meeting this one is. Simple conversations at the beginning of a meeting help people connect and make the transition from meeting to meeting. Some groups begin their meetings by asking everyone, "What do you need to say in order to be fully present at this meeting?" A quick once-around the room with everyone providing a response allows people to clear their minds, and they are able to bring their whole selves to the gathering.

Personal questions are powerful ways to deepen our connections. They make us uncomfortable, and they make us think. Why did you come to this meeting? Why are you staying? What are you willing to do to contribute to the success of this meeting? What are you not willing to do? What acts of courage will our work require of us? These questions get people's attention and set a different tone.

The best way to connect people to the purpose of your meeting is to ask the question (originally developed by Kathy Dannemiller), What do we want to be different in the world because this group of people met?

Discover the Way Things Are—Build a Shared Picture of the Current Situation

People carry stories in their heads about current reality and how we arrived at the present situation. The easiest way to discover the current situation is to ask people to share their stories. Or you may ask people to take a few minutes to write a story describing the organization today and then read their story aloud. The individual stories, taken together, reveal how the whole system operates. When people understand how the whole system operates, they become more willing to develop solutions that support the whole system operating effectively.

Elicit People's Dreams—Build a Shared Picture of Where You Want to Go

We've found the arts to be powerful tools for creating a picture of where people want to go. You don't need artistic talent, just the willingness to share a personal vision of the future.

For example, you might invite the members of your team to make simple drawings that capture an aspect of the future they dream of. Even crude sketches can carry powerful messages about the future. Writing can also uncover the future. Try asking people to imagine themselves five years in the future and spend just five minutes writing about what they see in a free-flowing, open-ended style. Many varied observations will emerge from this exercise, but in time, some common themes will surface. These themes represent the shared picture of the future, the goal toward which you will work.

Decide on the Future You Want to Create

The next step is to decide how you want to move forward. How you decide is important. If there is one thing that frustrates meeting participants, it is thinking they were in a participative decision-making process only to find out that only one voice counted: the boss's voice. The group must know ahead of time how it's going to make the decision. Many options are available, from the boss making the decision, to participants providing input and the boss having the final say, to consensus decision making. What's most important is that the method you choose is clear and everyone understands it.

Having made the decision, the next question is who will implement it. Again, you have many options. The leader can appoint people to be responsible for each task. Volunteers may be called for, perhaps by creating a sign-up sheet. A mixed method is to assign someone to lead a task and then have people volunteer to work on the task.

Attend to the End—Pay as Much Attention to Endings as You Do to Beginnings

"How people enter a room and how they leave a room is as important as what they do in the room." I was talking with an architect who was participating in creating a new hospital when he made this statement. If you don't want your meetings to end with a whimper, you need to put as much thought and attention into saying goodbye as you did into saying hello. In our work, we like to end by taking time to review decisions and agreements so that everyone is sure about the decisions and the next steps. Then we reflect together on the work we have accomplished. We ask people to identify what they appreciated about working with others. We don't rush the ending, nor do we drag it out.

Meetings are rituals that convey powerful messages. Designing meetings using the meeting canoe blueprint helps create new rituals that give your meetings the engagement edge.

KEY POINTS

▷ People resent not having a voice in changes that affect them, even if the result will benefit them.

▷ Everyday interactions are the basis for engagement.

▷ Find out what people care about by asking them what they care about at work and why.

▷ Support others in achieving their goals.

▷ Share what you care about by letting others know why you are willing to put your own time and energy behind an initiative.

▷ Meetings are the most overlooked fast-track engagement opportunity available.

QUESTIONS FOR REFLECTION

▷ To what extent do people's voices count in your organization?

▷ Do you know what is important to people in your organization?

▷ What would it mean if you treated employee goals as your own?

▷ To what extent do you share with the people in your organization why you personally care about a change initiative?

▷ What would you do differently if you treated everyday meetings as engagement opportunities?

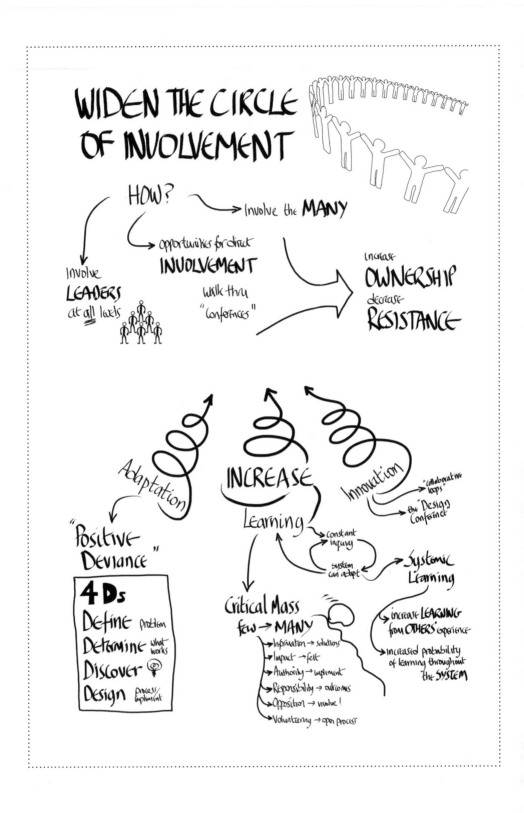

CHAPTER 6

Widen the Circle
of Involvement

Our local taxi service takes me to and from the airport. A few years ago the company installed a new computerized dispatching system along with new credit card terminals. On paper, it looked great: faster dispatch, improved cash flow, quicker and more accurate credit card processing. Drivers, customers, and the company would benefit.

The problem was it just didn't work. Drivers couldn't contact dispatchers; credit card processing was a disaster. Drivers kept their old manual imprint machines at the ready. Whenever it came time to pay my fare, I heard "If they had only asked us, we would have told them and saved all this BS." Lost productivity; frustrated, angry employees; disgruntled customers—this is the cost of not widening the circle.

Whenever you introduce change, you can be sure of one thing: there will be unintended consequences, such as drivers dispatched to the wrong places and credit card terminals that don't work as promised. You need everyone to pitch in and to make the new system work, not the moans and groans from friendly taxi drivers. Had the drivers been involved from the outset, they would have spotted potential problems and pitfalls. And because they owned the solution, they would have worked hard to implement it. What would you rather do: implement someone else's plan or implement a plan that you helped create?

PEOPLE SUPPORT CHANGE WHEN THEY'VE HELPED CREATE IT

In their classic 1948 article, "Overcoming Resistance to Change," Coch and French describe the impact of involving people in changes that affect them. Coch and French conducted experiments on the effect of involving employees in changing work procedures in a manufacturing organization. High-involvement groups, in which employees were involved from the beginning, not only outperformed the no-participation groups but also increased productivity, while the no-participation groups' productivity dropped and grievances and quits increased. The high-involvement groups also outperformed groups allowed to choose between predetermined outcomes. Today these results seem intuitively obvious, yet we often ignore the lessons learned from this landmark study. The earlier people are involved in the change process, the better.

Coch and French are not alone in reaching this conclusion.

Renowned social scientist Eric Trist said, "No one can force change on anyone else. It has to be experienced. Unless we invent ways where paradigm shifts can be experienced by large numbers of people, then change will remain a myth" (Weisbord and Janoff 2000, 22). Marvin Weisbord, who coined the phrase "getting the whole system in the room," further developed this concept. What he meant was involving all the various stakeholders of an issue in the deliberations about it. For example, in dealing with complex educational issues, this means including schoolchildren, parents, teachers, and local business and community leaders. In creating organizational futures, this means including employees at all levels, customers, suppliers, and community representatives (Weisbord 1987, 273).

WE'RE YOUR LEADERS—WE KNOW WHAT'S BEST

Douglas McGregor supports this point of view in his classic work on Theory X and Theory Y. McGregor (1960) states that the ability to create solutions to organizational problems is widely distributed throughout the organization. It is not the sole province of an elite few nor is it the province of the best and the brightest nor does it reside in the hierarchy. Rather, this capacity belongs to the entire organization. Involving the whole system to address systemic issues is at the heart of the new change management.

In *The Intelligence Advantage*, Michael D. McMaster talks about a leadership mind-set that works against widening the circle: "We become attached to our beliefs that we are leaders because we have titles . . . These attachments prevent us from showing the way by going first and they support the kind of thinking in which others need to change and we are fine; or these attachments deceive us into believing that we can create all the required change on our own. The worst outcome of this attachment is that we think we are able to know what to change and how to change it without including the rest of the system" (McMaster 1996, 77).

WE'RE YOUR LEADERS—HELP US PLAN THE CHANGE

In a situation quite similar to the one that Detroit Edison faced, a manufacturing organization had been working for over three years to redesign its workforce, with little to show for the effort. A highly engaged union-management steering committee led the change, but few other employees were involved. Recognizing that market factors could put the company out of business if the needed changes were not made quickly, the leaders decided to engage the organization in creating a new workforce design.

They used the Conference Model process to engage the whole organization through a series of three three-day conferences (250 people per conference) and then conducted smaller "walkthrus" for those unable to attend the conferences. Through the conferences and walkthrus, everyone had input into the new organization. In a few short months, the change process had moved from apathy to interest and from a few supporters to a critical mass of people who cared about the outcomes. Coincidentally, as this process unfolded, productivity began to increase and employees began to set new production records, even before they implemented any of the improvements they identified during the conference process.

WHAT ARE WALKTHRUS?

Walkthrus are a powerful way to widen the circle. Even if you involve a thousand people in your change process, if your organization has tens of thousands, you need to find a way to reach them. Walkthrus are one- to two-hour meetings or workshops for people who were unable to attend the actual conferences. Participants receive information about what is happening and then give feedback on the conference results. These sessions are highly experiential and critical to your success (Axelrod and Axelrod 1999).

WHY ARE WALKTHRUS SO POWERFUL?

We have seen over and over that walkthrus generate interest. When we first created the Conference Model, we thought all the power was in the large group conference. Now, after twenty years' experience, we are convinced the real power comes from combining large group interventions with the walkthru process. In one organization, nearly 500 people volunteered to attend a conference after the first walkthrus—an increase of 177 percent over the first conference. In another organization, 250 people in a 10,000-person organization were directly involved in the change process. The rest participated in walkthrus. An organizational survey asked, "Did you feel like you could contribute to the change process?" Eighty-five percent of the people surveyed said yes.

While nothing beats face-to-face conversations, social media provide a new platform for walkthrus. Organizations are using social media to make information readily available and keep the conversation going. People are using social media on their

---

HOW TO INCREASE OWNERSHIP
WHILE REDUCING RESISTANCE

- Involve the many in the change process from the very beginning.
- Provide opportunities for direct involvement through orientations, town-hall meetings, walkthrus, feedback sessions, social media, and large group conferences.
- Make sure that leaders at all levels of the organization are included in the process from the very beginning.

own to spread the word about what they like and don't like about current changes.

When you are thinking about whom to include, don't say, "They won't come." We were working on a project to improve access to services for addicts. The question came up, "Should we include judges from the court system?" The response was "They can't come. Their dockets are full." But someone said, "Let's ask them anyway and let them tell us." Judges did participate, along with police officers, teachers, counseling professionals, health-care providers, and people in recovery and their families. At the end of the process, a judge said, "As a result of participating, I've learned that I've been sentencing people in a way that works against recovery. I'll be sentencing people differently from here on out."

INCREASING INNOVATION, ADAPTATION, AND LEARNING

The old belief that organizations are linear, cause-and-effect-driven systems existing in static environments is outdated. Monetary crises halfway around the globe can cause shock waves in businesses across the United States and vice versa. We now measure the product life cycle in the computer industry in months instead of years, as organizations deal with constantly changing technology and fickle consumers. Worldwide health care is in constant flux as health-care professionals, hospitals, and patients and their families struggle to deal with a world of mind-boggling technological advances, changing patient expectations, and escalating costs.

Organizations are constantly seeking ways to adapt in order to survive in an increasingly turbulent environment. Moreover, organizations have to deal with multiple change initiatives simultaneously. It is common for an organization to be introducing new information systems, improving processes, and redesigning organizational structures while attempting to transform itself from a hierarchical silo-based organization to a cooperative team-based organization.

In *Harnessing Complexity,* Robert Axelrod—noted political scientist, game theoretician, and creator of the tit-for-tat theory (and my cousin)—and coauthor Michael Cohen explain that in a complex adaptive system, everyone's strategies influence the context in which everyone else is acting. "A system is complex when there are strong interactions among its elements, so that current events heavily influence the probabilities of many kinds of later events" (Axelrod and Cohen 2000, 7).

Axelrod and Cohen state that you harness complexity when you stop asking the typical cause-and-effect questions and begin asking a new set of questions, such as "What . . . agents [people or groups of people] and strategies are involved, and what interventions might create new combinations or destroy old ones?" (Axelrod and Cohen 2000, 20).

How to Ensure Innovation

Most people imagine innovation as the work of a lone scientist making a breakthrough discovery. That scenario is rare. Innovation occurs through exposure to new and different ideas. Working with people who are similar to yourself only reinforces your beliefs. Moreover, it turns out that even the most dedicated scientist who came up with a brilliant idea was not alone after all. He or she probably had thousands of conversations and shared experiments with others before coming up with the breakthrough concept.

Axelrod and Cohen (2000) explain that without variety, innovation and adaptation are unlikely. You can introduce variety into a system by providing opportunities for people who have varying points of view and strategies for dealing with issues to interact. Through these encounters, new ways of working emerge and the system eventually adopts them. Without this type of interaction—which can come only from widening the circle of involvement—innovation is not possible.

Everyone's concept of what is possible expands when people at all levels of the organization and important outside stakeholders such as customers, suppliers, and community officials are included. Discussing issues with those who are part of the same system but who have different perspectives sows the seeds of innovation. When change emanates from a single source (as with a top-down management style) or from like-minded people (such as groups of senior executives), the variety necessary for innovative thought is blocked.

Two Examples of Innovation Action

Here are two brief examples of innovation, one from our Collaborative Loops process and the other from our Design Conference.

Innovating with Collaborative Loops

In the Collaborative Loops process, dissimilar project teams come together to create their own change process using the four engagement principles. Variety is inherent when people no longer work alone. Teams gain clarity on their purpose, outcomes, and change strategy by receiving feedback from other teams in the room (Holman, Devane, and Cady 2007).

The Child Health Initiative team at Fraser Health Authority in British Columbia originally wanted to establish a central place where they could provide services such as immunization, vision and hearing testing, and counseling. To the team, this meant constructing a building that would cost millions of dollars. However, their thinking changed based on feedback from other teams in their Collaborative Loop: a mobile van that cost $150,000 could provide child health services. This van could take health services out into the community.

The team let go of the building idea when feedback from other teams in their Collaborative Loop indicated the building would probably go unused most of the time and parents would have difficulty bringing their children to a central place. With the help of the other teams in the room, the Child Health Initiative team developed the mobile van idea. Instead of spending millions, they spent thousands.

Innovating with the Design Conference

Here is how we introduce variety when redesigning processes and organizations. The Design Conference starts out by asking participants to design an organization based on a single criterion. We call this "single-concept thinking." Then new groups are formed to analyze the previously developed designs in terms of their positive, negative, and interesting aspects. They share their findings with the larger group to make the results of their analyses available to everyone.

Then participants join a third group to create a new design that uses the best of all the ideas and meets all of the criteria for the new organization. Notice how we are continually adding variety by having people meet in different groups as we also increase the discussion depth. Again, teams analyze design proposals and share the results with the total community. Groups adjust their designs, and the total community goes through a multiple-voting process to determine the final design.

To ensure that good ideas are not lost, we introduce a Treasure Hunt process: having chosen a final design, the participants identify features from the designs not chosen that they want to see included in the final design. This process makes sure good ideas are incorporated. In the end, everyone can see how his or her idea contributed to the final product (Axelrod and Axelrod 1999).

How to Ensure Adaptation

Adaptation refers to the ability of an organization to respond to rapidly changing conditions in its environment. Adaptation occurs when the various parts of the system come in contact with each other and either duplicate successful strategies or develop new strategies because of their interaction.

If you were to look at cases of terrorists who somehow managed to get onto planes, you would invariably see that information about them was somewhere in the system but was not shared in a timely enough manner. When we widen the circle of involvement, we create connections between people and ideas. These connections enable the rapid spread of information and allow the organization to respond to rapidly changing conditions. When interaction and communication funnel through silo command-and-control structures, adaptive processes die. Terrorists slip through when silos prevent information sharing.

A chemical products company recognized the power of information sharing when it involved customers and employees from all the components of the organization in creating a new product-development process. Because of their successful interactions in developing the new process, scientists from the lab, production people, and salespeople now routinely meet with customers to understand their needs and create new products. The organization is now able to adapt rapidly to shifts in customer requirements because both the scientists in the lab and the manufacturing people are fully engaged in product development. Previously, people believed that the only ones who had enough social skills to meet with customers were the sales force!

How to Ensure Learning

Since Peter Senge's book *The Fifth Discipline* (1990) came out, much has been made of "the learning organization." Learning occurs when there is constant inquiry about what is working and not working so the system can adapt to a constantly changing environment.

Learning is crucial to an organization's survival. What I mean by learning is not individual learning but the ability of the whole system to learn from its experiences and then use that learning to adapt to its environment. First developed by Jerry and Monique Sternin, the Positive Deviance (PD) process is a grand example of learning in action. The PD process helps a community identify and spread its own best practices. Positive Deviance reflects the belief that every system contains people doing the right thing. In this process, instead of experts telling people what the best practices are, people dialogue with each other to understand what is working and what keeps them from doing what they know works. They share successful strategies and decide together which ones they want to adopt (Positive Deviance Initiative n.d.).

POSITIVE DEVIANCE: A GREAT PROCESS
WITH A TERRIBLE NAME

"Deviants" in this case are not terrible people. Any organization or community contains people whose uncommon behaviors and practices have allowed them to find solutions to problems affecting everyone. These people work in the same situation and have the same access to resources as people who are not succeeding, yet they are successful. These folks are Positive Deviants. The Positive Deviance process seeks to identify successful people and their strategies. Then it goes on to create collaborative practices that enable everyone to create their own practices that work in their unique situations. Having people invent practices that work for them avoids the "not invented here" syndrome that often prevents the spread of best practices.

The Positive Deviance process consists of four Ds:

1. *Define* the problem and what a successful outcome would look like.

2. *Determine* through discovery and action dialogues if people in the system are already successful.

3. *Discover* the uncommon practices that successful people use by continuing the discovery and action dialogues.

4. *Design* a process that enables others in the organization or community to access and practice the new behaviors (ibid.).

Our colleagues at the Plexus Institute used the Positive Deviance process to reduce staph infections in hospitals. Aggregate data from three hospitals reporting data for intensive care PD pilot units documented a drop in hospital-acquired MRSA (methicillin-resistant *Staphylococcus aureus*) infections of 26 to 62 percent at participating hospitals (Plexus Institute 2009).

CREATING A CRITICAL MASS OF PEOPLE MAKES IDEA ADOPTION MORE LIKELY

Widening the circle creates a critical mass. Sociologists define "critical mass" as that group of people necessary for a whole population to adopt an idea. A critical mass can range between 10 and 30 percent of a population. As a society, for example we have gone from everyone having an ashtray in the home to outlawing smoking in public places. Before such a cultural shift could happen, a critical mass of the population had to come to believe that smoking was hazardous to everyone's health. This critical mass then influenced the rest of the population to adopt the new direction.

When you widen the circle instead of having a few champions, you end up with hundreds of champions. The change process moves forward with a life of its own, and leading change stops being a lonely activity.

WIDEN THE CIRCLE OF INVOLVEMENT TO GENERATE SYSTEMIC LEARNING

If you want systemic learning to happen, widening the circle of involvement is essential for two reasons. First, involving more

HOW TO CREATE A CRITICAL MASS OF PEOPLE

Creating a critical mass is about moving from the few to the many. Here are some guidelines about whom to include in a change process:

- *Information.* Include people who have specific information needed to create effective solutions. For example, include those who have specific knowledge about the introduction of a new information system.

- *Impact.* Choose people who will feel a direct or indirect impact from possible changes. For example, in a school system, include students in the process; in a business, include employees from the various units and functions.

- *Authority.* Choose people who have the authority to implement potential changes. For example, include the leader or leaders who must ultimately approve the recommended changes.

- *Responsibility.* Invite those who have responsibility for the outcomes of the changes. For example, include the supervisors and middle managers who will have operational responsibility for the proposed changes.

- *Opposition.* Invite those likely to be opposed to the new course of action. For example, include those who could lose their jobs as a result of the proposed changes.

- *Volunteering.* Don't handpick everyone who participates. People will think you are stacking the deck with those who will agree with you. Open up the process to volunteers.

people increases the opportunities to learn from others' experiences. Second, involving more people enhances the probability that learning will occur throughout the system.

Mercy Healthcare Widens Its Circle of Involvement

At Mercy Healthcare in Sacramento, California, my colleagues and I used the following approach to support learning as we implemented a new organizational design created using the Conference Model process. The problem facing us was that five hospitals needed to implement systemic and local changes. Some changes affected the whole organization and required concurrent implementation across the system, and other changes applied only to a specific hospital.

To facilitate learning, we created an implementation planning group. This group included key people from all of the systems and hospitals involved. We had a rotating membership so that the units or systems that were undergoing the implementation process had the most members, and those who had either already implemented the changes or were about to implement the changes had fewer members. This process allowed learning to flow from those who had gone before to those who were next.

We used large group processes extensively during the implementation process to adapt the redesign template to local conditions and to share experiences. The rotating membership of the planning group and the extensive use of large group conferences allowed groups to share learning as the implementation process proceeded. This in turn allowed the organization to adjust the implementation process to conditions that could not have been foreseen when the process began. Instead of sticking to a rigid plan, the organization adapted its plan as learning occurred during implementation. Improving patient access and flow throughout the Mercy Healthcare system could not have occurred without widening the circle of involvement.

WHY PREDICTING EVERY STEP OF A CHANGE PROCESS IS DOOMED

Change processes that lay out a clear path are seductive in that they promise a step-by-step approach with clear outcomes and results. They appeal to the common human need for predictability, order, and structure. However, when change processes do not build in mechanisms for self-correction and learning, they are doomed to failure because they do not provide for adaptation as the process unfolds. Dwight D. Eisenhower said it best when he described the planning process necessary for a military campaign. He said you must develop detailed plans for conducting the campaign and then be prepared to abandon them at a moment's notice.

An Air Force Base Widens Its Circle of Involvement

An air force base was in the midst of a major supply-chain improvement process. In spite of the fact that a consulting firm had sought the input of many people in the organization through committees and focus groups, deep pockets of resistance still existed. Project leaders needed something more. They had planned to release the project in stages, and for the major releases of the project they held large group sessions based on the four engagement principles. People met to learn what was going to happen, identify potential pitfalls, and identify solutions. Large groups included government contractors, air force and navy personnel, and union officials, as well as the consultants who were working on the project. The results were astounding. In the words of the lead consultant, "During our large group session we identified and developed solutions for all the issues where I thought the project was vulnerable. I wish we had had this kind of involvement from the very beginning. The whole process would have been a whole lot easier."

MANUFACTURING PLANT WIDENS ITS CIRCLE OF INVOLVEMENT—AND ACHIEVES UNANTICIPATED GOALS

A manufacturing plant in North Carolina was creating a team-based organization using the new change management. When it came time to decide whom to invite, the process planners included people from all levels and departments, customers, suppliers, and local community members. Because the plant was a major employer in the community, the planners decided to also include the president of the local chamber of commerce, bankers, state and local politicians, and a local environmentalist.

Inviting the environmentalist was the most worrisome for the planners. They perceived her as a rabble-rouser and a trouble-maker. At the beginning of the conference to create a vision for their work, they asked those present to share why they decided to participate. When the environmentalist's turn came, she spoke eloquently about the local river. She talked about how everyone used the river for recreation. People swam, fished, and had barbeques on the river banks. If you lived in the town, you loved and used the river. Yet the river was in danger. Pollution worsened daily. Pretty soon, you would be able to walk across the river. The people most contributing to this danger? Well, they were right there sitting in the room.

The stakeholders in the room were also mothers, fathers, aunts, uncles, cousins, and grandparents. Suddenly all of them realized what the river meant to them. They decided there and then that cleaning up the river would become a major part of the change initiative. They included being environmentally responsible in their vision for creating a team-based organization. But it didn't end there. Our activist rabble-rouser was not a single-issue person. As the work to create a team-based organization proceeded, she contributed ideas about how to improve teamwork within the plant and between the plant and the town.

Without the environmentalist's participation, pollution would have increased and the process of creating a team-based organization would have lost a major contributor.

KEY POINTS

▷ People support what they have a hand in creating. Eric Trist said, "Unless we invent ways for large numbers of people to experience paradigm shifts, then change will remain a myth" (Weisbord and Janoff 2000, 22).

▷ The belief that you can create all the vital changes by yourself is a barrier to widening the circle.

▷ Widening the circle produces many champions.

▷ New ideas grow when people with different points of view interact.

▷ Learning occurs when you continually inquire about what is working and what is not working.

▷ Widening the circle accelerates the ability to respond to turbulent environments.

QUESTIONS FOR REFLECTION

▷ Who else needs to be included? Whose voice is required?

▷ How will you introduce variety into your change process?

▷ What are you doing to support organizational learning?

▷ What innovative ways can you develop to widen the circle of involvement?

▷ How wide should your circle be?

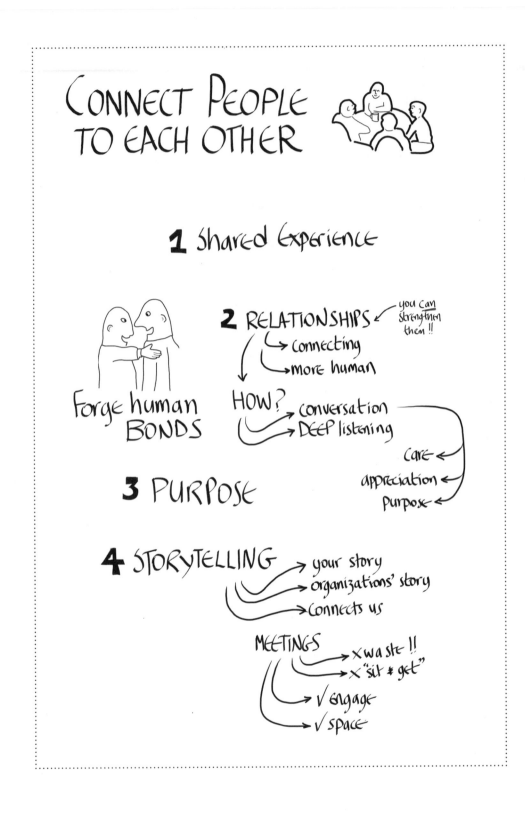

CHAPTER 7

Connect People to Each Other

Widening the circle of involvement brings more people into the conversation. But unless they are able to connect to the task and with each other, nothing happens. How can we connect people to each other?

FOUR BIG CONNECTORS FORGE HUMAN BONDS

Connection does not occur the same way for every person, nor does it occur the same way every time. Connection deepens through shared experience, as you strengthen relationships, because you share a common purpose, and through storytelling. Each opens a doorway to deeper connection.

Shared Experience: A Life-Changing Flood

The hurricane hits land. Swollen rivers overflow their banks. No electricity. No water. Sand covers what was once your living room. Two miles away, your car lies upside down. Trees sever rooftops, leaving cutaway houses. Your family album joins your neighbors' treasures in a debris-laden stream. You are homeless, without food, water, or a place to sleep.

Your neighbors check in to see if you are all right. They bring food and water, readily sharing their meager resources. You join others to lift a downed tree from the house on which it rests. A neighbor's boat takes an elderly man to the hospital over the washed-out roads. People who barely gave each other the time of day yesterday are now sharing food, clothing, and shelter.

Now imagine you look around a conference room and see a group of people you trust deeply. No matter what happens next, you know that the heartfelt connection you have with these people will never be broken. No matter where you are, a call from one of them will make you stop whatever you are doing and respond immediately. Whether you've shared a natural disaster or a traumatic workplace experience, you have an enduring bond.

The last six months have been pure hell. But the long hours, impossible deadlines, demanding leaders, and shifting customer requirements have forged connections that will last forever. There were knock-down, drag-out fights, times you thought the group would split apart at the seams, yet you did more than survive; you succeeded beyond everyone's wildest dreams. In the process, you became friends.

Shared experience provides a common bond. The bonds forged in the heat of battle are not easily broken. But your life does not have to be on the line for you to connect with others.

The Shared Experience of Struggle Even Binds an Authors' Group

I belong to the Berrett-Koehler Authors Cooperative, a group dedicated to supporting authors and advancing Berrett-Koehler's mission: creating a world that works for all. The shared experience that binds us is writing a book. We know what it's like to take an idea and make it into a book. We understand the trials authors go through as we seek to make public what is in our bones. We've been through the process, from submitting a proposal to holding the final edition. Because we share a common experience, we feel connected to one another.

The shared experience of working to improve an organization builds connections that last. Through these experiences, people get to know each other. As a result, day-to-day work becomes easier.

How Shared Experience Improved Cincinnati Bell's Service

Cincinnati Bell had a long-standing problem with directory assistance. It took three days from the time a person got a new telephone number to the moment it appeared in the operators' database—so for three days, the operators were giving out incorrect telephone numbers. This problem had been around for a long time. Each part of the system—the hardware manufacturer, software developers, database managers, and directory assistance operators—was aware of the problem, and each had tried to solve it. Unfortunately, these prior efforts had never involved all the component parts. The operators would work with the database managers, or the software people would work with the hardware people.

Then, during a conference to redesign the directory-assistance function, Cincinnati Bell brought all the relevant parts of the system together: representatives from the hardware manufacturer, software developers, database managers, directory-assistance operators, and customers were present. As they worked on creating a team-based organization, connections deepened and a solution developed within a couple of weeks. Now new numbers appear in the database within hours.

Relationships: You *Can* Strengthen Them

Many of us meet people and fail to remember their names. One reason for this is that we are not connected. That is why when we first meet others, we search for commonality. We ask questions like, Where did you go to school? Where have you worked before? Where are you from? With each question we hope to hit pay dirt, to bridge the chasm that separates us from the nameless faces that stand opposite us.

And then it happens. We find the connection. Someone in the group is from our hometown, another works in a similar field, and another has mutual friends. The iceberg of isolation begins to melt. Suddenly, we can remember their names. They have gone from being nameless faces to being real people. We have forged the tenuous first links of connection.

When we connect with people, we feel more human. We move beyond the isolation of our locked doors, gated communities, office cubicles, and organizational silos to unite with others. We are then able to do what none of us could have done alone.

Do Try This at Work

Conversation accompanied by deep listening builds connections. Here are three conversations guaranteed to build connection. All you need is a little curiosity and the desire to see the world through someone else's eyes.

1. *The care conversation.* Find out what the other person cares about and why. Share what you care about and why. When we ask people to have this conversation they don't want to stop talking because it is so engaging.

2. *The purpose conversation.* Ask, "What do you want to create? What will be different because this group met?" This conversation connects people about the future they want to create. It's much more energizing than problem-focused conversations.

3. *The appreciation conversation.* Let someone know what you appreciate about him or her. If you hear how others appreciate you, ask them how what you did was useful. This is not fishing for compliments. You'll be surprised what you learn.

Michael Gecan, in *Going Public,* speaks to relationships' importance when he says, "All living is *meeting,* not *meetings.* We don't take time to meet one to one with others, to hear interests, dreams, and fears, to understand why people do what they do or don't do what they don't do" (Gecan 2004, 21).

But when you know what other people care about, what they hope for, and what they are afraid of, you connect with them. Because you are connected, the work is easier. Yes, connecting with others takes time, but it is well worth the investment.

Purpose: What Drives You?

Teachers and their principal sat in a circle discussing the purpose for improving the school. As members of the team shared their personal reasons, they talked about the need to improve test scores, provide a better educational experience for students, and stimulate learning. They had held these conversations before. It is safe to say that most people tuned out as speakers droned on about the scores.

As the discussion bogged down, we probed deeper and asked why improving the school was important to each person. Suddenly, I noticed that one of the teachers had tears in her eyes. I asked her what was going on. She described a recent incident in which one student shot another student after school. The killing was even more shocking because the victim was a student who liked school, who got good grades, who wanted to make a better life through education. Through her tears, the teacher said, "Creating a safe school for learning is more than improving test scores and creating a new curriculum. It's about saving kids. That's what we're about. We're all about saving kids—the kid who pulled the trigger and the kid who was shot. That is the difference we have to make." Others in the group immediately grasped what she was saying. Their connections deepened as a result.

Chief information officer Chris Moore of Edmonton, Alberta, talks about the importance of purpose this way: "You need a purpose that is greater than just making change. You need something to drive you. What was driving me was my desire for my staff to have what I had: fulfillment in our work and freedom to take action. The drive to create fulfilling work came because when I met with people, they looked empty. I wanted to create a workplace where people felt good about themselves and their work" (C. Moore, pers. comm., November 9, 2009). As Chris's dream became reality, absenteeism dropped 25 percent and resignations dropped 36.7 percent. What makes these results even more outstanding is the fact that the organization's absenteeism and resignation rates were already below company and national averages.

Find a Noble Purpose

Shoji Shiba, winner of the MIT Deming Prize, believes that transformative change can occur only when what he calls a "noble purpose" exists. He wants to know, What is the contribution to society or the planet? Health care and education have a built-in noble purpose: maintaining healthy, productive lives and educating people to make the world a better place (S. Shiba, pers. comm., September 2, 2009). But as with the teachers in the previous story, achieving higher test scores is not a noble purpose.

Some organizations' products don't lend themselves to a noble purpose. But these organizations can find a noble purpose. They may decide to focus on the environment, like Patagonia, or provide time for employees to work in the community, like Timberland. Having a noble purpose gives meaning to what people do. As an IT person at Timberland said to me, "I could do IT anywhere, but I do IT at Timberland because of its commitment to the community."

For most people, saving $30 million from a hospital budget does not have meaning as a purpose for their work. They may recognize the need, but it does not create energy or excitement. However, improving health care so that doctors and nurses can care for people in the way they envisioned when they entered the profession has tremendous significance. A doctor talked with great emotion about his experience treating trauma patients in an emergency room. "The trauma cases became just pieces of meat to move along. I stopped seeing them as human beings. What we are proposing here—the organization's change strategy—will allow me to feel human again because I will be able to treat patients as human beings." Improving patient care reconnected him with his own sense of purpose.

YOUR PURPOSE IS NOT ENGRAVED
ON A WALL PLAQUE

Three words of caution:

- First, no written statement of purpose will engage people. Essential as it may be to write down a purpose, dialogue *about* the purpose engages people. Plaques on the wall do not engage people. In far too many instances, plaques are silent testimony to failed change processes.
- Second, you cannot create meaning for others. People must be able to find meaning in the purpose for themselves. A purpose that is meaningful to you is not automatically meaningful to others.
- Third, the way you create purpose is just as important as the purpose itself.

Storytelling: How Did Our Organization Come to Be the Way It Is?

In *Leading Minds,* Howard Gardner (1995) states that organizations have stories about themselves: we accomplish what we set out to do; we are customer oriented; we pull together in a crisis; we're smart, creative people; it's dog eat dog around here; we never implement anything; or people in this organization are unreliable. He goes on to state that organizational change is a process of shifting the story an organization has about itself. To shift the current story, you must first understand the story in place and how it came to be.

CONNECTED BY THE STORY OF THE ACCIDENT

The story began innocently enough; we were conducting a large group session to redesign an organization. We asked the participants to discuss successful events from their past and events that caused regret. A voice from the back of the room said, "There was the accident." So I said, "Could you tell me about it?"

It had been awful. The boiler exploded and debris shot into the plant. Joe, Billy, and Ronnie were in the line of fire. Joe and Billy lost their legs, and Ronnie suffered permanent brain damage.

As the story unfolded, people talked about the colleagues who risked their lives to save the threesome. They described how good it made them feel that ten years later, people from the plant still take turns visiting Ronnie, how even now, Joe and Billy get a helping hand when they need it. They described how this accident made everyone realize safety is the number one priority. Today you don't have to worry about leaving the plant with the same number of body parts you had when you entered.

This story's connecting power was in helping people throughout the plant understand the importance of safety. It was especially important to newcomers who often thought people were obsessed with safety and could not understand why.

MEETING IS MORE POWERFUL THAN TWEETING

In today's organizations, people may work together for years without ever meeting. Their communications consist of voice mails, e-mails, tweets, and texts. Walls, cubicles, and organizational silos reinforce people's isolation. When they need to get something done, they do not know where to go or whom to ask. This lack of connection supports the silo mentality and the negative stereotypes about that "other" department, the one that can never get its act together.

Even proponents of social media state that high-tech communications work better when the participants have established a relationship prior to using them.

WHY "SIT AND GET" MEETINGS DON'T PRODUCE CONNECTION

A common frustration for leaders is the silence that comes when they ask for questions after making a presentation. Announcing a new direction does not launch the initiative. People need time to chew on it, digest it, and make it their own.

Here is a typical scene. The leader talks from the podium, PowerPoint slides at the ready. People are seated auditorium-style to receive the word. Forty-five minutes later, the leader finishes and asks for questions. Stony silence follows. This silence is not the result of a poorly developed vision but of a failure to connect with the audience.

Consider this alternative. A leader needs to engage her organization in significant changes. She follows the advice in chapter 6 and widens the circle of involvement to include those who have information, authority, and responsibility, as well as those affected by the proposed changes.

The meeting starts with people at the tables introducing themselves to each other, talking about their hopes and concerns regarding the proposed changes. Table by table, people share the results of their discussion.

The leader then shares her story about the need for change, and she outlines possible courses of action. The table groups then spend time discussing what they heard and identifying key questions. What follows is a lively question-and-answer session along with a discussion of the issues.

The meeting closes with people feeling energized. Even those who may not agree with the direction feel included in the change process and feel that their concerns are valid and understood—not because they've been manipulated into feeling good but because they have been included and their concerns have been recognized.

FIRST AID FOR "SIT AND GET" MEETINGS

1. Avoid Death by PowerPoint at all costs. Cut in half the number of slides you plan to use.

2. Limit presentations to no more than twenty minutes.

3. Seat people at round tables.

4. Provide the opportunity for people to discuss what they just heard. Two great questions are, What did you hear? and, What do you want to know more about?

5. Table by table, ask people to report on one thing they heard from you and one thing they would like to know more about.

6. Close by providing people with next steps. This does not have to be a detailed list but rather what people can expect following this meeting.

THE MEDICAL INSURANCE STORY: HOW ALL FOUR CONNECTORS WORKED TOGETHER

Imagine you run a major health-care provider processing thousands of patient claims a month. First you must determine if each claim is appropriate. Whenever a standard or practice changes, the physicians have to approve the changes and the legal department must review them. IT then updates its programs to reflect the latest practice guidelines. Finally, all of the claims supervisors and examiners receive training on how to use the new review policies.

Making incorrect medical policy decisions creates problems with regulatory bodies, increases costs, and decreases member satisfaction. Creating and implementing a process to ensure the smooth and timely execution of medical policy changes is essential to the organization's success.

Five attempts had already failed to design and implement a process that would enable claims examiners to apply the appropriate medical policy changes. Learning from past mistakes, a new team composed of a physician, an organization development (OD) consultant, and an ace project manager decided to use an approach that fully engaged the organization in the change process. Working with a planning group that represented a microcosm of the organization, they designed a large group conference, including sixty participants from all the stakeholder groups, including physicians, attorneys, system programmers, claims supervisors, and claims examiners.

Storytelling

The large group sessions began by encouraging conversations in which participants could get to know each other. At table groups, people answered questions such as, Why did I come to this organization? and, Why do I stay? These conversations enabled the participants to connect to each other as people, not as functions that typically argue with each other on the phone. Many of these people had worked together for years but had never actually met. The energy in the room began to rise.

Purpose

Next, the CEO spoke to the participants about why this effort was so critical to the organization, how it would affect customers, and how it could improve staff satisfaction. He spoke from his heart, and he let them know how much he was counting on their wisdom and dedication.

Shared Experience

Then the group had a conversation about the current state of affairs. The group used a map of the current process to show people the way the work was currently organized, where hand-offs and delays occurred, and where disconnects proliferated. This was eye-opening for everyone involved. The reactions ranged from "Yep, that's how it is" to boisterous laughter at the inanity of the process. Then the group listened to various customers of the process tell about their frustrations as well as their requirements for a successful process. Seeing the map and hearing from the customers had a profound impact on the participants. They had a total commitment to redesigning the process and a shared sense of purpose for making the implementation successful. Now it was time to go to work.

The group came back together for the second day of the conference to draft the workflow for the desired state. With

Post-it notes, flip chart paper, and markers they created a new approach to drafting and implementing new medical policies. They represented all of the customers' and stakeholders' views in the design and built the process around meeting customer requirements.

Relationships

When the participants reflected on their experience, they expressed satisfaction at their ability to have candid, nonblaming conversations. But most importantly, they expressed their willingness to be a part of the project after the conference and make the implementation a success. One physician participant reflected: "When we started, you had sixty people who came into the room hating each other. When we left, you had sixty people in the room who did not want to leave and volunteered to be a part of the implementation. I'd say the approach is working."

Connectors Kept Everyone Together for the Hard Work

The truth was that the work so far had been successful, but the process had just begun. The project manager and subteam leaders created a detailed plan to implement the workflow changes that came out of the conference. The plan included organizational reporting relationship changes, technology and system changes, and behavioral and skill changes. Subproject teams composed of conference participants and other stakeholders executed the work detailed in the project plan. Leadership stayed engaged throughout the process.

Outcome: Connected Teams Produced Remarkable Results

Within six months, the organization saw demonstrable results. By the end of the first year, its people had reduced the process cycle time by 75 percent. They increased the number of policy changes made annually from 2 to 186. Finally, they achieved more than 80 percent customer satisfaction with the outcomes of the process redesign. The redesign effort was successful because the process allowed people to understand what prevented them from meeting customer needs and to develop a shared sense of purpose for improving the way they worked together.

You can have great results if you apply the four connectors. Align around a compelling purpose. Connect people through the shared experience of working on something they care about. Build relationships through conversation. Use stories to discover the way things are and to elicit people's dreams.

KEY POINTS

▷ Unless you are able to connect people to the task and with each other, nothing happens.

▷ The first connector is shared experience.

▷ The second connector is relationships.

▷ The third connector is purpose.

▷ The fourth connector is storytelling.

QUESTIONS FOR REFLECTION

▷ What is the story of your organization?

▷ What was your experience your first day at work in this organization?

▷ To what extent do you feel connected to your organization's purpose?

▷ What is the current state of relationships in your organization?

▷ How can you go about creating shared experiences in your organization?

CHAPTER 8

Create Communities for Action

In community, people do together what none of them could do alone.

Cirque du Soleil is a leader in its field and is a community at its core. W. Chan Kim and Renée Mauborgne, authors of *Blue Ocean Strategy*, identify Cirque as a Blue Ocean Strategy exemplar. Blue Ocean companies redefine their industry. In doing so, they make the competition irrelevant by changing the rules of the game (Kim and Mauborgne 2005).

What Cirque did was transform the circus by eliminating the most expensive parts of the show. No longer were there three rings and animals. Now there were acrobats, music, spectacular sets, and most importantly, the show.

A Cirque performance is a stunning artistic experience. If you have ever been to a Cirque show, you know what I mean. If you haven't, the next time you have a chance, see a Cirque performance. You'll immediately understand.

Kim and Mauborgne suggest that Cirque owes its success to its Blue Ocean Strategy. I argue that Cirque's success has its roots in community. Cirque du Soleil lives and breathes community. Gaetan Morency, vice president of global citizenship for Cirque, describes the organization this way:

We tour together. We live and work together. We are like a traveling tribe. We have long-term relationships.

There is a tension when you live and work together. We can have fifteen to eighteen nationalities in a show. There are problems when you bring people together from different nationalities. They have different values about how they raise their children, treat their spouses. You have to find ways to live and work together. That is what community is all about.

Everything is about commitment to creating the best show possible. There is emotional, tangible connection to the show. At the end of the show, there is applause. You get immediate feedback; then you go back to living with your coworkers.

Human beings are at the center. Our core business is the people on stage. We put creation front and center. This is very important to artists. Our expertise is creation and people. After that comes the customer. Everyone is committed to the show.

The purpose of our community is creating the best shows in the world. This is a tough organization: if you don't fit, the organization will turn you out. You gain citizenship at Cirque through the values you share. (G. Morency, pers. comm., December 17, 2009)

BUT WHAT IF YOU'RE NOT CIRQUE DU SOLEIL?

Most organizations do not live and work the way Cirque du Soleil does. Generating community is different in a touring company than it is in a customer service unit. But Cirque's leaders work in ways that can sharpen our own understanding of community in an organization. We can apply the principles extracted from the Cirque experience in our own ways.

WHAT MAKES *CIRQUE DU SOLEIL* A COMMUNITY

- Creating a compelling purpose—creating the best shows in the world.
- Putting people at the center—recognizing that without people, there is no show.
- Valuing differences—having fifteen to eighteen nationalities represented in one show.
- Encouraging dialogue—committing to open communication, asking tough questions, and allowing free-flowing information.
- Unleashing talent—encouraging performers to help create the show.
- Committing to the communities where you work—understanding the impact they have on the communities where they play.
- Giving back—contributing 1 percent of gross revenues to the community (ibid.).

Henry Mintzberg called community the social glue that binds us together for the greater good. "Community means caring about our work and our colleagues, and our place in the world, geographic and otherwise, and in turn being inspired by this caring . . . A vibrant community [is one] where talented people are loyal to one another and their collective work, everyone feels that they are part of something extraordinary, and their passion and accomplishments make the community a magnet for talented people out of schools or working at other places" (Mintzberg 2009, 2). Cirque du Soleil certainly fits this description. Other organizations can and do.

COMMUNITIES DON'T JUST HAPPEN

Whether a group becomes a strong community can seem whimsical, a matter of fate. It doesn't have to be that way. The desire to become a community of people willing to act must come from within. Although leaders can foster conditions where community is possible, they cannot mandate community. Much like a farmer who grows a crop, the leader can till the soil, plant the seed, and provide irrigation but cannot make the seed grow.

Here are seven proven strategies to create the conditions under which communities are ready and willing to act.

Strategy 1: Create a Compelling Purpose

Cirque's compelling purpose is to produce the best shows in the world while being the neighbor and employer of choice and making the world a better place. Organizations committed to improving the world achieve more than those with a vision to just beat the competition, write David Rock and Yiyuan Tang in the *NeuroLeadership Journal* (2009).

When people in your organization come together to take the hassle out of work or tackle important issues like health care and sustainability, they are creating their own compelling purpose. At the same time, they activate the brain's reward state. Your status increases because you are working on something larger than yourself. Autonomy increases because you see the possibility of taking action. Relatedness increases as you work with others to achieve something larger than yourself. Remember that increasing status, autonomy, and relatedness increases the reward state, which in turn increases collaboration and innovation (Rock 2009).

A compelling purpose looks to the future. Have you noticed that when you are about to make a change in your life, you see that change everywhere? For example, if you are about to buy a house, the world seems full of For Sale signs. If you are about to buy a car, you suddenly see new cars everywhere. If you are thinking of having a baby, you see babies and pregnant women everywhere. What is going on? In our minds, we have a picture of the future we want to create. Suddenly our brains let in information that has always been there but we were unable to see. This new information shows up as possibilities, and we are motivated to take action. We know the future we want to create, see the possibilities, and act.

In *The Path of Least Resistance for Managers,* Robert Fritz (1999) states that when people know what future they want to create and understand their current reality, they create "structural tension." Structural tension is the difference between the current state and the desired future. When you know your car needs replacing and have a picture in your mind of a new car, you experience structural tension. Normally, people resolve this tension by moving toward the desired future. In other words, a future orientation creates action.

Table 8.1 shows several examples of compelling purpose.

TABLE 8.1
EXAMPLES OF COMPELLING PURPOSE

Organization	Compelling purpose
Kaiser Permanente—Diablo Service Area	Being the best place to work, best place to receive health care
Berrett-Koehler Publishers	Creating a world that works for all
Calgary Health Region	Building bridges, tearing down walls

A word of caution: while the purposes I've identified read well, they are only a nice start. A purpose becomes compelling through dialogue that helps people make sense of the purpose. When the purpose makes sense to people, they act.

QUESTIONS TO CREATE A COMPELLING PURPOSE

- What will be different in the world as the result of your work together? To what end? In order to do what?

- Why do you care? Why are you willing to put your own time and energy behind achieving this goal?

Strategy 2: Put People at the Center

Allstate's Customer Enterprise Services (CES) is a six-thousand-person organization spread over eighteen locations. CES provides IT support to Allstate's call centers and back-office functions. It handles half a billion customer transactions a year. CES's internal and external customers were dissatisfied with the service they received. CES was under immense pressure to improve service while reducing cost.

Today the CES community is blowing away its budget, coming in millions of dollars under plan. Postcall interaction surveys measuring billions of interactions from customers found that satisfaction increased from 77 percent to 84 percent within seven months. Allstate realized a fifteen-fold return on investment within a year and a half.

John Bader, vice president of CES, talks about "turning over the organization to the organization . . . Inclusion was and remains a major organizing principle. We based our efforts on the work of Judith Katz and Fred Miller. We needed to create a safe environment. Everyone's voice counted. We honored differences. We developed a clear line of sight between the inclusion behaviors and our desired results" (J. Bader, pers. comm., September 1, 2009).

The community came together in what Allstate called "waves." The waves were composed of the maximum mix (max-mix) of people from the organization. In max-mix, hierarchy and organizational structure blur as people from all functions and levels work together to improve the organization. The meeting canoe (chapter 5) carried the community through the waves. Putting people at the center enabled innovative solutions to emerge.

"Once you get the idea of max-mix, people start to get it and they want to go from there . . . All you have to do is ask. And you have to make it safe [for participants] to answer. When you hear uncomfortable things, you need to have this attitude: 'Thank you very much, may I have another?'" (ibid.).

Strategy 3: Value Differences

Kraft Foods' introduction of new SAP software with harmonized business processes provides an excellent example of creating communities for action. Introducing SAP across the total business in North America—and region by region, across the globe, to ultimately impact 40 percent of Kraft's 110,000 employees—required the creation of many communities. Before the change process began, Jan Mears, director of change management for the Catalyst Program at Kraft, described the coming change this way: "Our sales force will all be operating with new handheld tools using SAP software. People driving trucks will be using new technologies. People working in customer service centers and the finance community will all be working with SAP. If you conduct any transactions in the HR world, you're going to be doing it in SAP. It'll go across the business" (J. Mears, pers. comm., October 30, 2009).

Jan created three different types of communities to figure out how to bring change to the multiple, diverse organizations that make up Kraft. The first was the advisory group, which blends senior people in the affected business unit with people from the Catalyst extended leadership team. The advisory group meets regularly with project leaders to discuss the upcoming changes, the impact on the business, and how they will work with their business and their people.

Changes to processes like order-to-cash cut across traditional organizational boundaries. So Catalyst needed a second community. This multilevel multifunctional group comprises what the technology world calls "key users." The group's role is two-fold: it serves as a communication conduit during implementation, both providing information to the organization about the change and getting information from the organization in order to make local adaptations to the process. The change network conducts face-to-face and virtual meetings where people talk about what the new world will look like, what it means in terms of how to move forward, and what changes they need to tackle as a group. They also use social media such as Web sites, blogs, and wikis to enable discussions that leapfrog traditional functional hierarchy. The change network in turn builds a community of people who will be using the new process who can then share ideas with one another.

Annually, Jan convenes a third community. Members include the leaders of the change networks, systems, project management, and organization development in what she calls the "Change Summit." In this community, people share what they've been doing, address issues of common concern, and learn from each other.

Throughout, Jan and her team were aware of and valued the differences in the communities where they worked. While it is true that people around the world share many similar aspirations, living and working in Jakarta, Indonesia, is different from living and working in Northbrook, Illinois (ibid.).

While you may not be implementing something as complex as the conversion to SAP at Kraft Foods, the communities Jan created help people make sense of the change effort, communicate across boundaries, and learn from each other throughout the change process.

Strategy 4: Encourage Dialogue—the Super Glue for Relationships

I think about dialogue as the conversations needed to build and strengthen a community. In the beginning, you might encourage discussions by asking questions such as,

- Why did you decide to attend?
- What do you want to create for yourself as a result of being here?
- What do you want to create for the organization?
- Why did you join this organization?
- Why do you stay?

As you seek to understand the way things are, you might ask,

- What is our story about the current state of affairs?
- What conditions give rise to the story?

To elicit people's dreams, you might ask people to create a future they believe in. The arts can be used to elicit people's dreams. Writing, drawing, and performing skits are great ways to unleash people's dreams.

To solidify commitment, you might ask,

- What do we have energy for doing individually and collectively?
- What do you want to have happen?
- What are you willing to do to make it happen?
- What are you not willing to do?
- Who needs to do what?

Strategy 5: Unleash Talent

Every community contains passionate people with ideas about how to improve the community. For three consecutive years, the National Association of Business Resources named West Monroe Partners one of Chicago's "101 Best and Brightest Companies to Work For"—an award that recognizes excellence in corporate culture and innovative human resources practices. Crain's *Chicago Business* and *Consulting Magazine* also have recognized West Monroe Partners as a best place to work (West Monroe Partners n.d.).

West Monroe Partners unleashes talent through its chiefs program. In the chiefs program, any employee who has energy or passion for an idea can make it happen. Chiefs at West Monroe Partners do everything from convening book clubs to tackling the stickiest business issues. There is a chief cleaning officer, a chief green officer, and a chief holiday officer, to name a few. Chiefs also tackle traditional business issues such as business development and project management.

To start a chiefs program initiative, all you have to do is identify the need, write a charter, and submit it to the "Chief of Chiefs." Once your charter is approved, you get a budget and can proceed. The next step is recruiting other members for your team. Paulette McKissic, director of human resources, describes the chiefs program this way: "We use the chiefs program in recruiting to describe the way we encourage talent. People learn about it during orientation, and they experience it every day. What stemmed from a need to develop leadership and ownership in the organization has blossomed into a key differentiator for us" (P. McKissic, pers. comm., February 11, 2010).

Strategy 6: Commit to the Communities Where You Work

Commitment is one of the defining characteristics of a community that cares and is willing to act. To quote a line often attributed to Goethe, "Until one is committed, there is hesitancy, the chance to draw back, always ineffectiveness."

When people commit to a course of action, they are willing to hold themselves and others accountable. They are willing to put forth extraordinary amounts of time and energy to reach a common goal. Committed people take action. They are not ineffective, they are not hesitant, and they produce results. Everyone knows that commitment is important, but what does it take to produce commitment?

Commitment occurs in the mind, the heart, and the hands.

Logic-driven commitment occurs in the mind. In this case, the facts create commitment. When organizations create the case for change, the goal is to provide a convincing set of facts that will cause people to commit.

Heart-driven commitment starts with relationships. I become committed because an individual or group I know, respect, or admire asks me to become involved. I commit to action primarily because of my relationship with the individual or the group. Personal values drive heart-driven commitment. If a change is consistent with my own values, then I am likely to commit to it. Examples include supporting Mothers Against Drunk Driving, improving public schools, working with youth, improving customer service, or being part of a high-performance organization.

Jonah Lehrer, in *How We Decide*, writes, "Since Plato, philosophers have described the decision making process as either rational or emotional: we carefully deliberate, or we 'blink' and go with our gut . . . Our best decisions are a finely tuned blend of both feeling and reason—and the precise mix depends on the situation" (Lehrer 2009).

Hands-driven commitment is a result of personal experience. After Hurricane Katrina struck the Gulf Coast in 2005, my wife, Emily, and I volunteered to rebuild houses in Mississippi. Our decision to go to Mississippi was both rational and emotional. We knew the facts and deep in our hearts, we wanted to make a contribution. As we worked with others to make a difference, our daily experiences deepened our commitment. We were on our hands and knees removing flooring. We tore down walls. We built new walls. We stood on scaffolds as we finished drywall. We listened to devastating stories. We ate together. We sweated together. We prayed together. At the end of the day, we were physically and emotionally exhausted. Community's bonds, deep commitment to each other and to the task, arose from these experiences.

THREE STEPS TO GAINING COMMITMENT

1. Share the facts.
2. Speak from the heart. Tell people why you are willing to spend your own time and energy on what needs to be done.
3. Create opportunities for the community to come together and be successful.

In his essay about the benefits of civic engagement, "Bowling Alone," Robert D. Putnam (1995) states that engagement occurs when we establish common ground and trust our neighbors. When we develop connections with people, we trust them. Because we trust them, we are willing to work in community with them.

The mistake most leaders make when they seek to gain the commitment of others is employing a single strategy. They mistakenly believe that once people know the facts, they will commit to making the necessary changes. Or they believe that emotional appeals will win the day. This view is only partly right. Since you don't know what will appeal to whom, it is important to provide the facts, speak from the heart, and create experiences where commitment grows.

Many see commitment as a binary choice: someone is either committed or not committed. Another way to view commitment is as a continuum, reflecting degrees of commitment from passive to active engagement. As shown in figure 8.1, there are five levels of commitment.

FIGURE 8.1

THE FIVE LEVELS OF COMMITMENT

Consider the levels in detail:

1. *Not getting in the way.* People are silent but are carefully watching what is going on.

2. *Providing resources without personal involvement.* People are willing to provide funds or share the credibility associated with their name, but they are not willing to do anything that requires any effort.

3. *Personally participating.* People are willing to participate personally in the change.

4. *Taking a stand.* People are willing to work actively to advocate for the change process and to involve others in the process.

5. *Taking high personal risk.* People have something personally at stake and are willing to take a stand.

Strategy 7: Give Back

Vibrant workplace communities give back to the communities in which they reside.

Cirque gives back 1 percent of its revenues to communities. Not 1 percent of its profits, 1 percent of its revenues. This means that giving back comes before profits, not after.

Service sabbaticals give Timberland employees time to commit their special skills to the nonprofit organization of their choice. Sabbaticals can last anywhere from two weeks to six months. In 2007, Timberland employees invested more than 500,000 hours of service to create meaningful change for children, families, and the environment. Timberland even provides a Service Toolkit on its Web site so that anyone can plan and execute a community event (Timberland n.d.).

Cirque and Timberland give us examples of how to give back on a large stage. But giving back can also occur on a small stage. We had just completed a strategic planning conference for a local school district involving more than 250 teachers, staff, parents, students, local citizens, and community leaders. Part of the strategic planning process included student-led input on the stresses and strains of being a student in a community where high expectations are the norm. Within weeks of our completing Vision 2020, two high school students in the district committed suicide.

The school and community leaders mobilized community-wide discussions on teen suicide. Learning from their Vision 2020 experience, school leaders convened all facets of the community. They provided support and comfort and learned from each other as they identified ways to prevent future tragedies.

COMMUNITY BOUNDARIES CREATE FREEDOM

At first glance, the notion of putting limits on a community seems to be overly restrictive. But without boundaries, you die.

Your skin is a boundary between you and the outside world. It forms a container for your organs. Your skin is permeable, casting off sweat and taking in harmful chemicals if you don't wear protective clothing. It is not a rigid boundary. It stretches and bends as it protects you from everyday bumps and bruises.

In a similar manner, a community needs boundaries so people in the community know who is in and who is out, what is open for discussion and what is not. Communities can become too restrictive when they keep out people who have every right to belong. They can become too porous when they open the floodgates of participation. It is not uncommon in disasters for the word to go out asking people not to come to the disaster zone. As surprising as it may seem, this boundary is necessary when the community cannot incorporate more help. More help only adds to the chaos. When the situation settles down, more people can enter the community.

In organizational change, boundaries help people focus their energy. Here are some examples of useful boundaries:

- Our goal is to bring better and more creative solutions to the customers at a faster rate, be an industry leader, and enable us to grow our business profitably. We do not anticipate job reductions, nor are job reductions a goal.
- The new organization we are creating must be capable of
  - Seven percent improvement in process reliability
  - Reduction of controllable cost by $15 per unit of output
  - Improvement to the 98 percent level on the customer-satisfaction survey
  - Creation of a world-class safety environment

- If you propose changes to the labor agreement or company policy, we will refer these ideas to the labor management negotiating team or company officials as appropriate.

KEY POINTS

▷ Community allows you to do together what you cannot do alone.

▷ "A vibrant community [is one] where talented people are loyal to one another and their collective work, everyone feels that they are part of something extraordinary" (Mintzberg 2009).

▷ Remember the seven strategies for creating conditions where community can thrive:

1. Create a compelling purpose.
2. Put people at the center.
3. Value differences.
4. Encourage dialogue.
5. Unleash talent.
6. Commit to the communities where you work.
7. Give back.

▷ Boundaries create freedom

QUESTIONS FOR REFLECTION

▷ How many communities do you belong to?

▷ What defines these communities?

▷ What makes them work?

▷ What workplace communities need attention?

▷ What will increasing community at work require of you?

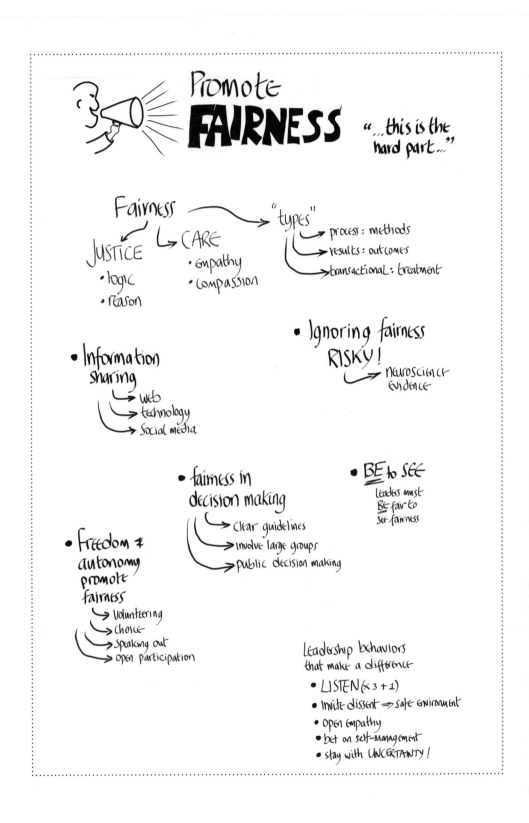

Promote **FAIRNESS**

"...this is the hard part..."

Fairness → "types"

JUSTICE → CARE
- logic
- reason

CARE
- Empathy
- Compassion

"types"
- process: methods
- results: outcomes
- transactional: treatment

- Ignoring fairness RISKY!
  → neuroscience evidence

- Information sharing
  → web
  → technology
  → Social media

- fairness in decision making
  → clear guidelines
  → involve large groups
  → Public decision making

- BE to SEE
  Leaders must BE fair to SEE fairness

- Freedom & autonomy promote fairness
  → Volunteering
  → choice
  → Speaking out
  → open participation

Leadership behaviors that make a difference
- LISTEN (x 3 + 1)
- Invite dissent ⇒ safe environment
- open empathy
- bet on self-management
- stay with UNCERTAINTY!

CHAPTER 9

Promote Fairness

This is the hard part.

The new change management's success rests on everyone's willingness to embrace fairness. Without fairness, you can widen the circle of involvement, connect people to each other, create communities for action—and still fail. Change processes that don't seem fair appear only to serve the interests of the elite. When this happens, change never gets off the ground and your organization ultimately fails.

Notions of fairness go beyond people's experience with a particular change process. They extend into the organization as a whole. Fairness is the hallmark of productive societies. For example, the concept that everyone is equal under the law is enshrined in the United Nations Universal Declaration of Human Rights. Patently unfair practices such as Bernard Madoff's misdeeds and Enron's deceptions outrage us all. The growing unease about the disparity between CEO salaries and the rest of the organization's paychecks infuriates people who believe in proportionate compensation. The inequality in health care throughout the world causes people to stop, think, and act.

FAIRNESS: DO YOU PROVIDE IT, OR DO PEOPLE DEMAND IT?

The VIA Institute in Cincinnati studies character strengths in all societies. Researchers break fairness down into two parts: justice and care. Justice emphasizes logic—as in balancing the scales of justice. Care emphasizes empathy and compassion— the ability to stand in someone else's shoes. When people think about fairness, they usually think about it this way:

- Process fairness—are the methods used fair?

- Results fairness—is the outcome fair?

- Transactional fairness—Are people treated fairly as policies and procedures are implemented?

Whenever anger about the lack of fairness boils over, people take action.

Laborers took to the streets to form unions when employers treated them without a modicum of decency. The unfairness they resented—and changed—included fourteen-hour days with pay for only eight hours, child labor, deadly working conditions, and poverty wages. The forty-hour week, a safe working environment, and health care for workers are measurable hallmarks of an equitable working environment. Thanks to these earlier achievements, people now seek fairness in other aspects of their working life.

IGNORING FAIRNESS IS A RISKY PROPOSITION

Remember our lessons from neuroscience? When people sense unfairness, it triggers the threat response in the brain and they close down. Creativity, collaboration, and productivity vanish as everything begins to unravel. In contrast, the brain's reward

---

FAIRNESS GUIDELINES

- Minimize or eliminate the privileges that come with roles and titles.
- Create decision-making processes where people know their voice counts.
- Create opportunities for everyone to participate in the change process to the extent he or she desires.
- Include fairness as part of your decision-making process. Ask the questions, Are our proposed changes fair? How will this impact people?
- Create an approach that includes everyone and exempts no one.
- Take experts off the pedestal. Everyone has knowledge. Everyone can contribute.

---

state ignites when people believe actions are fair (Rock 2009). When you widen the circle of involvement, connect people to each other, and create communities for action, you increase people's sense of fairness. When you promote fairness as you apply these three principles, you get a multiplier effect that enhances the whole.

An equitable, fair organization makes the difference between a follow-the-rules, resistance-prone organization and an organization where people grasp the issues and initiate action.

FAIRNESS IN INFORMATION SHARING

The World Wide Web, social media, and even e-mail have dramatically changed the way we give and get information. The other day we were having a family discussion about penguins in Antarctica when my six- and eight-year-old grandsons, Andy and Zach, said in unison, "Just Google it, Grandpa." A world of information is just a keystroke away.

Simple e-mail has democratized organizations. No longer do formal chains of command restrict communication. You can talk to whomever you want, whenever you want. In many organizations, you can correspond directly with the CEO, an act previously unthinkable. Add Facebook, Yammer, Twitter, LinkedIn, and other forms of social media, and everyone now has the ability to share information within and beyond the organization. Some organizations even promote social media as a way to break down the organizational wall. We are in a shakeout period where people are trying to figure out how to use these processes effectively. However, you can be sure of one thing: social media have taken fairness a giant leap forward.

Senior managers often wonder why the rest of the organization does not see matters the way they do. Often it is because the rest of the organization does not have access to the same information as senior management. Is it any wonder that decisions appear to be capricious when some of us have information that others don't? I recognize there are times in organizational life when leaders do not share information for legal or competitive reasons; despite this fact, information sharing is an untapped organizational resource.

Sharing information is more than just making knowledge available. People also need to make sense of it. Not everyone takes in information in the same way. People work through their denial about what needs to be changed at different rates. That is why you need multiple opportunities and methodologies for information sharing and dialogue. Information sharing is not a one-time event, nor is it ever accomplished through one medium.

Informed Nurses Cut Patient Call Response Time by 87 Percent

Recently, a group of nurses learned during a large group conference that it was taking them an average of eight minutes to respond to a patient's call. What they learned prompted them to take decisive action. Following the large group conference, the nurses met on their own and developed processes and procedures to rectify the problem. Within a month, these nurses had reduced the average time to respond to a patient's call to one minute!

When information is public, individuals are able to analyze the information and make their own decisions. They are able to examine the facts of the situation and come to their own conclusions. They are not dependent on the analysis and interpretations of others. Public information is the cornerstone of independent thought and action.

FAIRNESS IN DECISION MAKING

One thing that makes people angry is thinking they had a voice in a decision only to find out later that there was one decision maker: the boss. At first glance, it may seem like providing decision-making guidelines limits fairness. In fact, clear guidelines increase fairness.

Guidelines let people know how to focus their energy. If you are announcing a new direction and they have no opportunity to influence the direction, tell them the truth. If you are presenting a new initiative and want input but you will make the final decision, people need to know that as well. If you are willing to let the group decide, that is important information too.

A feature of large group interventions is public decision making. When decision-making processes are public, all witness them. When people are part of the decision-making process, they come to their own conclusions about how well the process worked. Fairness is present and trust increases.

HOW FREEDOM AND AUTONOMY PROMOTE FAIRNESS

Freedom and autonomy are integral to the new change management. When people volunteer to be part of the change process, they are expressing freedom and experiencing fairness. Their

---

WWII FOOD RATIONING: SUCCESS RELIED ON SHARED DECISION MAKING

During World War II, Kurt Lewin worked with anthropologist Margaret Mead to identify ways of reducing consumption of rationed foods. In one instance, an expert lectured housewives on the need to change their buying habits. In another instance, experts gave the housewives the facts and time to discuss the issues, after which they made decisions as a group. The results are not surprising. People in groups that reached consensus through discussion changed their buying habits more than those in groups that received expert information through lecture. In consensus groups, the decision-making process was open, it was public, and it included everyone's input. Lewin (1948) identified a simple but telling principle: *we are likely to modify our own behavior when we participate in problem analysis and solution and likely to carry out decisions we have helped make.* In other words, information sharing coupled with an equitable decision-making process produces action.

participation is not dependent on their supervisor's approval. Everyone in the organization has an equal opportunity to participate in the process.

When people provide input on issues that affect them, they exercise freedom and experience fairness. When they speak out, discuss different points of view, and feel understood, they experience fairness. When they volunteer to take action, they experience fairness. Even when people choose not to participate, they experience fairness.

LEADERS MUST BE FAIR TO SEE FAIRNESS

Leaders are responsible for changing their own behavior first if they expect others' behavior to change accordingly. Their behavior change becomes a guide to action for others. They must also withstand the pull of the organization for them to act in more traditional ways that sabotage fairness. Success requires everyone in the organization to shift to new behavior patterns.

What leadership behaviors make a difference?

- *Listen, listen, listen, and when you can't stand it anymore, listen some more.* The heart of fairness is respect for opposing points of view. Listening creates understanding, builds rapport, and creates trust. When leaders listen, they do more than show respect for the other person. They implicitly share power by saying that the other person's point of view is of equal value to their own. When you do not listen to opposing points of view, you are saying that there is only one person whose voice counts—yours.

- *Create a safe enough environment by inviting dissent.*

- *Make statements like "If I were in your shoes, I'd be worried," "What concerns do you have?"* Or ask people to name the top ten reasons why your idea won't work. Everyone will watch how you respond. If the environment is unsafe, vital ideas and opinions go underground. If the environment is safe, ideas come forward and creative solutions emerge. Fairness prevails when it is safe to dissent.

- *Bet on self-management.* Do not do for people what they can do for themselves. Create conditions where people can act on what is important to them and watch them flourish. Change your role from controlling outcomes to creating conditions that encourage self-management.

- *Stay with uncertainty.* Do not abandon the process at the first moment of fear and uncertainty. Do not fall back to what is safe and sure. Stay with the uncertainty of the moment. Support fairness in the midst of chaos, confusion, and even conflict.

CHOOSE CHANGE PROCESS TEAMS LIKE JURIES

Fairness is the basis of the U.S. jury system. We trust that a random group of people can deal with complex legal issues and determine guilt or innocence. Like any system, our jury system has flaws. But despite occasional errors, our trust in the system remains intact. If we can trust the very foundation of law and order in our society to this system, why can't we bring that same spirit to the workplace?

What if we chose people to serve in change processes the same way we choose people to be on juries? Everyone in the organization would be eligible to participate in the change effort. We would assign slots to various stakeholder groups. People would be randomly selected from the various constituency pools to fill those slots. Everyone in the organization would be obligated to participate in the change initiatives that occur during the course of organizational life.

In this way, those determining new change strategies would represent a cross section of the organization. They would represent the various levels of interest in the process. A random selection process would ensure representation of all points of view in the process—not just those who were predisposed to go along or those who might benefit, but everyone.

At the heart of this proposition is the concept that organizational change is part of everyone's job—a right and duty of corporate citizenship, if you will. Everyone knows that it is the right and obligation of all U.S. citizens to serve on juries. Citizens who end up on juries take that responsibility very seriously: they do not take lightly the power to take away someone's freedom or inflict financial penalties.

I believe that if all employees everywhere knew that at some point in their organizational career they would be involved in shaping the course of the organization, three events would happen. First, we would have better-informed employees as they learn about the issues the organization faces. Second, a single constituency would no longer control change processes. Shared power would develop. Finally, because all employees would know that they would be on both sides of the change equation—sometimes as a developer and sometimes as a recipient—people would take the obligation seriously. They would consider not just the necessary changes but the impact of those changes on everyone in the organization.

EVEN DOWNSIZING CAN BE A FAIR PROCESS

Managers of a change process that involved downsizing from fourteen senior leadership positions to seven senior leadership positions took this novel approach. All fourteen leaders assumed they would be among the seven who lost their jobs.

Next they determined the notification plan and process that management should follow. What they came up with was striking in its simplicity.

- Each person should have a conversation with his or her boss as soon as possible. That conversation would begin with the person's finding out whether he or she had a job in the new organization.

- If the answer were yes, they would then go on to talk about the job and the roles, responsibilities, and expectations that came with that position.

- If the answer were no, the person would receive feedback about the decision and then hear whether other jobs were available in the organization or whether he or she would have to look for other employment. The boss would help the affected leader develop a strategy for job hunting inside or outside the company.

- Everyone would receive training and other assistance to ease the transition.

The results of this process were that seven leaders lost their jobs. Some stayed at their same level; others took jobs at lower levels. Still others took on different jobs within the organization.

At the start of a change process where downsizing was inevitable, the planning group designed a fair process for retraining and outplacement. Even though people did not like the downsizing process, they felt that the process for dealing with those who would be worse off was fair and reasonable. As a result, during the change process, many people offered up ideas and strategies that suggested the elimination of their own jobs! This unusual behavior occurred because the process passed the fairness test.

When you employ the principle of fairness, you balance the power in organizations. You do not eliminate hierarchy, but you level the playing field and allow more people to participate. The principle of fairness looks at power as an unlimited resource—something shared and distributed throughout the organization rather than hoarded and controlled.

FAIRNESS PAYS

Berrett-Koehler, my publisher, has the mission of "Creating a World That Works for All." For everyone at Berrett-Koehler, this is more than a slogan. Berrett-Koehler seeks to treat authors, employees, suppliers, sales partners, and all of its other stakeholders fairly. I know this firsthand through my experiences as an author, as a consultant to Berrett-Koehler, and as the authors' representative on the Berrett-Koehler Board of Directors.

In the first part of 2009, Berrett-Koehler's sales, like sales of nonfiction books throughout the U.S. publishing industry were down nearly 30 percent because of the global economic downturn. But unlike most of the rest of the publishing industry, which immediately turned to layoffs as a way to cut costs—with the decisions generally made behind closed doors by small groups of top executives—Berrett-Koehler turned to employees at every level of the organization to collectively work out responses to the sales shortfall.

We on the board were more than concerned about the future of the company. We peppered Berrett-Koehler management with questions about industry trends and company finances. At the same time, we were extremely proud of Berrett-Koehler management for staying true to the company's stated values during a crisis.

Leaders reviewed the company's financial realities as well as industry data in open company meetings. All employees participated in discussing the implications of that information and alternative options for responding to the bad news. A set of principles (mirroring principles that had been followed in previous challenging periods) were agreed upon by all staff for guiding the response to the sales shortfall, including "priority is given to honoring all written and verbal agreements" to all stakeholders, the company's mission and strategies would guide responses, and "all employees should participate in identifying and implementing sales-boosting and cost-cutting actions."

Staying true to the company's core purpose, people knew that whatever actions they took had to work for everyone. After much open analysis in which all employees voiced their views, the entire staff agreed to avoid layoffs (which would have placed the burden on a subset of employees) and to instead involve all employees in cutting compensation costs:

- A temporary 10 percent salary reduction for all but the lowest-paid employees
- No bonuses for any employees (including management)

While no one liked having his or her compensation reduced, employees saw the decision and the process for arriving at it as fair. Employees then mobilized to find other ways to cut costs as well as to increase sales. The result? Berrett-Koehler was able to get sales moving up again, to cut even more costs than projected, and to end the year with a profit after starting the year with a substantial loss.

At Berrett-Koehler, the cost-cutting process was fair, the way people were treated as they identified and implemented the solution was fair, and everyone agreed the decisions were fair.

KEY POINTS

▷ Ignoring fairness is a risky proposition.

▷ Ask the process fairness question: Are the methods used fair?

▷ Ask the results fairness question: Is the outcome fair?

▷ Ask the transactional fairness question: Does fairness exist as you implement policies and procedures?

▷ Apply the fairness test to decision making and information sharing.

▷ Increasing autonomy increases fairness.

▷ Trust people to make fair decisions for the good of the whole.

QUESTIONS FOR REFLECTION

▷ Are the methods you use fair?

▷ Do these methods result in fair outcomes?

▷ Do people experience fairness in your organization?

▷ Does fairness play a part in information sharing, decision making, and providing autonomy?

Words of caution
THREATS!
to beware of...

1 Different rules
↳ top leaders
↳ the rest of the organization

2 Disengaging conversations
↳ attentive listening
↳ Straight talk
→ Intentionally listen for
  • the HISTORY
  • THOUGHTS
  • FACTS
  • FEELINGS
  • INTENTIONS
  ...again
→ deeper/greater understanding of "RESISTANT" people

3 I count / you don't count
↳ bring other work into meeting
→ arrive LATE/leave EARLY
↳ crush/squash input

4 Past organizational damage
↳ Start by assessing damage
→ sceptical/cynical?
→ hurt?

5 Thermometer Solutions
↳ reactive
✗ get to the root cause

6 Loss of will
↳ high visibility increases • resentment
                          • frustration

7 "Collective folly"
↳ separation/fragmentation
→ proving what we already know
→ tradgedy of polarized groups
→ illusion of agreement

9 SHADOW ~~SHADOW~~

• Let go
↳ prerogatives
→ controlling decision making
↳ NOT ABDICATION

• More chaotic!
→ messy
→ appear confusing
→ LEADERS live with ambiguity

• Attracts attention!
↳ in the open
→ increased visibility
→ increased pressure

8 Impulse to manipulate
↳ People "feel" like they have a voice
→ dismiss others
↳ builds resentment

• Bigger investment
↳ costs
→ pressure

CHAPTER 10

When Engagement Disengages

SOME WORDS OF CAUTION BEFORE YOU BEGIN

This is the "buyer beware" chapter. When the new change management goes wrong, you are actually worse off than if you'd never started. At least one of nine threats usually causes the derailment. These threats deserve examination before you begin a change process so you can avoid getting in your own way. All ten are rooted in self-deception.

Self-deception is at the heart of the *shadow,* a concept from psychologist Carl Jung. As you seek to project a positive image of yourself, you may be unaware of your own shadow: the negative aspects of yourself that you would just as soon not consider.

Your shadow can be the desire to control others, to manipulate outcomes, or to win at any cost. You can suffer from the delusion that you already lead with an engagement edge. Rather than seeing yourself as needing to change, you believe others need to change. You can become trapped in the organization's expectation that, because you are the leader, you already know how to lead with an engagement edge. You always get the executive summary or "short course"—when you may require as much education and training as others—or more.

Beware of these threats to the change process:

1. Different rules for different folks
2. Disengaging conversations
3. I count/you don't count behaviors
4. Past organizational damage
5. Thermometer solutions
6. Loss of will
7. Collective folly
8. The impulse to manipulate
9. The new change management's shadow

Leaders are often surprised when distrust permeates their efforts to engage the organization. What they fail to recognize is the impact of their behavior. When people express dissatisfaction, they are holding up a mirror to you. They are telling you what they are—and are not—getting from you. Leaders often perceive this reflection as flawed, a distorted view of reality like one of those carnival mirrors that make tall, thin people look short and fat. This mirror is reflecting back to them their shadow side.

THREAT 1: DIFFERENT RULES FOR DIFFERENT FOLKS

When leaders' behavior shows that there is one set of rules for senior leaders and another for the rest of the organization, they violate people's sense of fairness.

It's hard to lead a community in which you don't participate. Leaders who kick off a meeting or workshop and then go on to do other tasks, only to return at the end of the session to bless the outcomes, are a classic example. They justify their behavior by saying, "People won't be honest in front of me." Meanwhile, their absence engenders mistrust about the leaders' true intentions and the importance of the group's own efforts.

Leaders who show up midstream are another example of different rules for different folks. Feeling their time is limited, they hurry to influence the change process. They fear that without their input, people will make serious errors in judgment. Not knowing what preceded their lightning visit or what is to follow, they act like the proverbial bull in the china shop, making comments out of context and damaging the process.

You sully fairness when you ask people to change and you remain unaffected. It is one thing to ask people to change, knowing that your job and role are secure; it is another thing to participate equally with people in the change process. How many projects have asked organization members to redesign processes and structures while exempting senior leadership from the process? How many leaders rest secure while asking organization members to potentially reengineer themselves out of jobs? What if leaders and organization members shared the same vulnerability during organizational change processes?

THREAT 2: DISENGAGING CONVERSATIONS

The failure to listen disengages. An alternative called "attentive listening," builds engagement. Sherod and Phyllis Miller originally described attentive listening in their book, *Core Communication* (1997).

"Understanding first, agreement second" is attentive listening's core principle. First, understand the other person's point of view. There is always time to disagree. However, when you try to reach agreement without understanding, you miss important engagement opportunities. Once you get into a debate, each person trying to win the other over, the ability to learn information that could actually improve the change process rapidly diminishes.

Here are six pointers for becoming an attentive listener:

- *Start with intentionality.* Listening for understanding creates trust and safety. Listening so that you can convince someone to come to your side produces defensiveness.
- *Listen for the history.* What has happened in the past that has caused people to think or feel the way they do?
- *Listen for thoughts.* People's personal experience colors how they interpret the same set of facts. Just look at recent controversies surrounding our political leaders to recognize how people can look at the same set of facts and come to widely different conclusions.
- *Listen for facts.* Facts are the raw, verifiable data.
- *Listen for feelings.* Listening for feelings means being able to understand and even to some extent experience the feelings of others.
- *Listen for intentions again.* Now listen for other people's intentions again. Learn what they want. When you come to understand their intentions, you will understand why they are saying what they are saying and doing what they are doing (Miller and Miller 1997).

Attentive Listening in Action

You have just presented your case for change to a group of employees and you are fielding questions from the floor. A hand goes up and a belligerent voice says, "I think you guys are just manipulating us!" Your first impulse is to kick the guy out of the room. Your second is to convince him of the rightness of your cause. You take a deep breath and say to yourself, "What do I really want to have happen here?" A voice from within says, "I want to understand why he feels the way he does." So you respond by saying, "You seem upset. Could you tell me why you feel that way?" He answers, "Damn right I'm upset. This is the fifth reorganization we have had in the last five years, and nothing gets any better. All that happens is that we move people around, and all we get from management is broken promises."

You respond by saying, "I think if I were in your shoes, I would feel the same way. In fact, I'm not satisfied with what we've done in the past." He replies, in a calmer voice, "We have plenty of problems around here, but no one ever asks us what to do about them. I would like to see the organization improved, and I have some ideas." You encourage him: "We need your ideas, and I hope that you will join us and help us turn this organization around." And he says in a quiet voice, "Well, maybe I'll try it this time."

Through attentive listening, you came to understand the fear and anger that the belligerent fellow in the audience was expressing. You avoided the temptation to punish the speaker or to try to convince him that the new plan would work when others had failed. Your only intention was to listen and understand the speaker's point of view. You therefore turned a potentially explosive situation into a positive opportunity. You helped a disengaged person take one small step toward engagement.

Conversations That Engage

A companion to attentive listening is straight talk. Together, attentive listening and straight talk build trust, which leads to engagement. Straight talk means sharing your own thoughts, feelings, and intentions in a way that allows for the expression of the other person's thoughts, feelings, and intentions. Straight talk respects the other person's point of view. Through this information sharing, new possibilities emerge. Straight talk and attentive listening create possibilities, while conversations that exclude these critical dimensions shut down possibilities.

Carol Gray, who was senior vice president northeast portfolio of Calgary Health Region at the time of the patient-centered care redesign (chapter 2), understands the importance of listening and straight talk.

> In the beginning, there was a high degree of skepticism. We were concerned we'd go through all this trouble and nothing would ever happen. Defining that approval process for the conference outcomes and really making sure that we had thought through the next steps reinforced the credibility.
>
> Being honest was important. When we were able to say, "You know what? We can't promise that it all will be approved and there'll be money, but we're certainly going to give it our best shot," it freed up everyone.
>
> We were worried about going out on a limb. There's always that little reservation that people will say, "Well, I don't know what was so great about that. We spent three days with you and what do we have? We have a nice document and nothing else to show for our work."
>
> There were a lot of those reservations at the beginning. I remember my partner on the project gasping, thinking about the financial support required, wondering aloud, "Is this the best use of the money that we have?" Taking physicians, nurses, and staff away from the practices was no small undertaking.
>
> We were pretty keen to try something more innovative. We knew we needed input in some fashion and this really was a novel approach. It was still a gamble in our minds. (C. Gray, pers. comm., September 10, 2009)

Attentive Listening Can Help You Understand Resistant People

If you practice attentive listening and create structures where attentive listening can occur, you will gain a new understanding of those you have been labeling as resistant. You will create the conditions for engagement. Also, you will gain information that will inform you about how your strategy may need to change in order to be successful. Listening deeply, without the intention to change another person's point of view, will allow new possibilities to emerge.

You might argue that this level of listening takes more time than you have. My response is that you can spend the time in listening and creating engagement or you can spend the time in dealing with a disengaged organization. The choice is yours.

THREAT 3: *I COUNT/YOU DON'T COUNT* BEHAVIORS

Engagement is an open conversation of possibilities. Disengagement is a one-way conversation of selling and coercion.

The following are examples of I count/you don't count behaviors:

- Bringing other work into a meeting
- Texting, surfing the Web, and answering e-mails during meetings, phone calls, and Web conferences
- Talking over, interrupting, and otherwise squashing input
- Arriving late and leaving early
- Creating hierarchical seating arrangements and office space that indicate who counts and who doesn't

THREAT 4: PAST ORGANIZATIONAL DAMAGE

By now, nearly every organization has tried to introduce change by using some form of employee participation. Typically, these efforts start out with great fanfare, only to fade when the next change initiative begins. With each new change, hope grows anew: This change process will really make a difference. This time someone will really involve us in a meaningful way. Disengagement rules the day when people learn firsthand that expediency trumps engagement.

Confronting organizational damage is essential to the success of the new change management. Have past attempts left organization members feeling resentful over dashed hopes and broken promises, or are they optimistic about the possibilities because of past successes? What caused success? What led to failure? While the new change management can help repair organizational damage, you must begin the new change management by assessing the current level of damage.

It is impossible to overemphasize the extent to which violations of trust, lack of fairness, and a leader's inability to listen disengage people and damage an organization. Likewise, it is astonishing how effective it is to genuinely reverse these behaviors. Here is a real-life example.

Brutal Honesty Helps a Hospital Bury Skepticism

A hospital was about to adopt the new change management to improve patient care. Focus groups signaled the start of the process. The purpose of the focus-group interviews was to identify those forces within the organization that supported the change process and those forces within the organization that could prevent success.

One important finding was that employees did not trust senior leaders. Employees believed that they did not get timely, complete information, and senior leadership did not tell the truth. Employees were skeptical about senior leaders' commitment to implement the changes they would recommend. They felt that previous attempts to involve them in change had been fruitless; they did not see what was different about this process. Employees experienced their good ideas as disappearing into a Bermuda Triangle.

Recognizing that these feelings would lead to disengagement rather than engagement, the senior leaders developed a strategy to increase trust: being brutally honest. Straight talk was the watchword. The leaders became fanatical about keeping their commitments. In those few instances when commitments needed revision or changing, the leaders communicated effectively with the organization about what changed and why they were unable to keep their commitments. They then developed new action plans with those affected by the change.

Over two years, the leaders have worked diligently to apply the principles and practices of the new change management. Their results: increased patient satisfaction, improved clinical quality, and reduced costs.

THREAT 5: THERMOMETER SOLUTIONS

A thermometer can tell you when there is a problem. For example, when your child's thermometer reads 102 degrees, you know something is wrong, but you don't know the cause. Engagement surveys lead to thermometer solutions when leaders try to fix the problem without talking to the people who completed the surveys in the first place.

Remember our leaders who threw pizzas at the organization in hopes of improving employee recognition scores? Had they talked with people in order to understand why they responded to the survey questions the way they did, the result would have been different.

THREAT 6: LOSS OF WILL

Consider the following scenario: A company has used the principles and practices of the new change management. Its managers have engaged large numbers of their employees, customers, and suppliers in creating a new way of doing business. In fact, business is so good, it is a problem. The company is growing so fast that one of the biggest problems now facing the organization is making sure that everyone gets a desk and a telephone.

Meanwhile, a dark cloud looms on the horizon. Members of the leadership team are struggling to keep their heads above water as market demands for their services increase exponentially. Soon they begin to resent the work the new change management requires. Meeting attendance is sparse. Frequently canceled meetings become the norm. Leaders complain aloud about the time and effort the change process requires. Slowly, the process grinds to a halt. The leaders soon abandon the change process that had successfully engaged their organization. They no longer have the will or the willingness to implement the process. Disappointment, disillusionment, and disengagement take over.

High Visibility Increases Risk If You Abandon a Change

When leaders use the new change management, they must think through the implications of their choice. Because the new change management widens the circle of involvement, the change process becomes highly visible.

Halting a change initiative involving the few leaves the few disheartened, but the organization can continue to function. Damage is worse when you have involved hundreds or thousands of people in a change process, only to have it disappear off the radar screen.

In the company cursed by success, the leaders did not start out intending to stop in midstream. But the excitement generated by the process soon turned to resentment.

These leaders will first have to overcome the distrust before starting their next change initiative. Had they taken a few minutes to understand the magnitude of the change they were undertaking, and examine whether they had the time and energy to follow through, there might have been a different result.

THREAT 7: COLLECTIVE FOLLY

I agree with Alan Briskin and his coauthors of *The Power of Collective Wisdom*, when they state, "Groups can be avenues for wisdom or unwittingly fall into traps of collective folly." Following the new change management's principles helps guard against foolish decisions. In the end, you must guard against collective folly by making sure everyone's voice is heard. Briskin and his coauthors (2009) warn against seeing the other person or group as the problem (for example, "I present my thoughts forcefully while you are hopelessly opinionated"). And they caution us to watch out for false agreements (agreements where people shake their heads yes, while their behavior says no). A paragraph does not do justice to this topic, but I wanted to make you aware of it. Briskin and his coauthors have much to say about the trap of collective folly.

THREAT 8: THE IMPULSE TO MANIPULATE

Prospective clients sometimes approach us saying, "We want to do something that makes people feel as if they have a voice in the future." The statement reveals the impulse to manipulate. *Feeling as if you have a voice is altogether different from actually having a voice.* This may seem like a trivial semantic difference, but it is not.

When potential clients come to us with this type of request, they are usually saying something like, "We already know what we want to do. We have the answers. We want to develop a process whereby employees feel as if they were involved and created the outcome. But what we really want is for people to come up with an answer that we have already determined." When leaders manipulate, they send the message that you have nothing to contribute. Most people resent that idea.

THREAT 9: THE NEW CHANGE MANAGEMENT'S SHADOW

Every change process has its positive and negative attributes. My enthusiasm for the new change management may well suggest that I see no negative aspects—but perfection is no more true of the new change management than of any other human system. Its warts must be visible for all to see.

Four Negatives of the New Change Management

The new change management has four negative attributes:

1. *It is more chaotic than other paradigms.* When more people are involved and the decision-making process opens up, the situation by its very nature gets messy. Other change

processes try to guard against feelings of chaos by limiting the involvement and decision-making authority of those involved. The new change management embraces the chaos and confusion that occur when we include more people and points of view. Successful implementation requires leaders who can live with the ambiguity that is inherent in the new change management.

2. *It requires leaders to let go of prerogatives.* This means letting go of decisions that are often seen as reserved for leaders only. It is sometimes difficult for leaders to move from developing the answer to identifying the elements that would make up a good solution. It is a leap for some leaders to stop handpicking every person who will be involved in creating change and move to identifying the skills and qualifications necessary for people to participate. It is hard to ask yourself the question, Is this something about which I actually have to make the decision, or can this decision be delegated to others?

   I want to be very clear. I'm not talking about abdication. I'm talking about letting go enough to deeply engage the organization in setting new directions. Some describe the experience of using the new change management as a course in learning how to let go without abdicating.

3. *It requires a bigger investment.* As the number of people participating in the change process increases, the initial costs increase. These costs are more visible than the hidden costs of dealing with the resistance generated by the old change management. Thus they often create pressure for quick results because of the huge up-front investment. This pressure for results often causes leaders to take shortcuts or to try to compromise the principles of the new change management.

4. *When the change process moves out from behind closed doors into the light of day, it attracts attention.* This increased visibility puts pressure on leaders and those designing the change process. Scrutiny sometimes causes people to abandon the principles of the new change management in an effort to protect themselves against criticism by creating outcomes that are more predictable. Change process leaders have to make sure that their behavior and the design of the change process stay congruent with the principles of the new change management. When leaders design processes or behave in ways that are incongruent with the new change management, they disengage the very people they want to engage in the process.

CAN YOU MANDATE A PARTICIPATIVE PROCESS?

At first glance, it seems wrong to initiate participative processes like the new change management in an authoritarian manner. Yet there are good reasons for doing just that.

Everyone knows that when leadership is serious about something, there is plenty of direction. Therefore, when you introduce the principles and practices of the new change management, you must introduce them in a way that is consistent with the existing culture. On one hand, people must see what you do as a break from the past. On the other hand, what you do must have the elements of toughness, control, and direction that let people know you are serious.

Therapists call this process "matching the system." For a therapist to induce change in a family, for instance, the family must regard the therapist as both part of the system and different from the system. If you want to move from a predominantly authoritarian culture to a participative culture, you must use authoritarian behaviors.

Warner Burke, author of "On the Legacy of Theory Y" in the *Journal of Management History*, describes it this way: "The paradox seemed to be that the more 'participative management' was launched in a participative manner, the less it became rooted and actually practiced. It was as if in order to take hold and gain traction, 'participative management' needed to be introduced in a command-and-control manner, highly top-down" (Burke forthcoming).

There is an additional irony. It seems that the more participative a leader is, the more people will accept authoritarian behavior when the leader chooses it. The more authoritarian a leader is, the more distrustful people are of participative moves.

The lesson here is that you need to be both part of and different from the system you seek to change. Do not shrink from being directive when you begin integrating the new change management.

HOW BRITISH AIRWAYS MANAGED A CHANGE USING FREEDOM WITHIN FRAMEWORKS

Neil Robertson, principal human resources business manager at British Airways, was facing a problem. BA was about to embark on an organizational change that would require reorganizing the HR function. "I remember being concerned that if a solution was devised by a small number of people in one small room, would it be the right solution, and even if it were the right solution, would they be capable of implementing it?" recalls Neil (N. Robertson, pers. comm., July 28, 1999).

The HR leadership decided to use the Conference Model to engage the HR organization and its internal customers in redesigning the HR organization to meet the needs of the future. Since that time, the HR organization has continued to employ the new change management principles as it supports change throughout the entire BA organization. I spoke with Neil about his experience in a wide-ranging conversation in which he shared what he has learned over the past five years.

Here are Neil's insights about using the principles of the new change management and dealing with the threats to success: "In the beginning, there needs to be informed consent by the leadership. They need to understand the potential, the risks, and the benefits. They need to be deeply involved in the boundary discussions, the number and diversity of people that will be involved in the process, and what it will take to maintain the operation while this change process is going on."

Building in short-term success is essential. Neil commented, "If you overload the change process and try to do too much, then the change process loses focus. People get discouraged because they do not see progress."

With regard to promoting fairness, Neil said, "People need to be respected for their knowledge and contribution. If they do not feel respected, they disengage. Leaders have a high-level view of the work in their organizations. However, they do not have a good understanding of the detail of what goes on. If you want to have successful change work processes, then you must involve, listen to, and respect the ideas and contributions of those doing the work. Also, transparency—making everything visible—is essential. We have used displays and information boards as a way for people to both understand what was going on and to provide feedback."

Near the end of our conversation, Neil commented on what he saw as a by-product of the new change management: "I think managers do not know it all, and they have to find ways to tap into the knowledge of the organization. Getting the system talking to itself in useful and systematic ways is crucial to success. When we are successful, we find that, in addition to bringing about organizational change, we have increased the capacity of both leaders and their organizations to handle change. This may be the most important outcome of all."

KEY POINTS

▷ When the new change management goes wrong, you are actually worse off than if you never started.

▷ When self-deception occurs, disengagement follows.

▷ Straight talk and attentive listening are the antidotes to disengagement.

▷ Beware of these threats to the change process:

1. Different rules for different folks
2. Disengaging conversations
3. I count/you don't count behaviors
4. Past organizational damage
5. Thermometer solutions
6. Loss of will
7. Collective folly
8. The impulse to manipulate
9. The new change management's shadow.

▷ Even the new change management has its own downsides.

QUESTIONS FOR REFLECTION

▷ Where does self-deception live in your organization?

▷ How are you sabotaging your own efforts to engage the organization?

▷ What could you do to ensure that your current change initiatives fail?

▷ When and where can you start practicing straight talk and attentive listening?

▷ What are the upsides and downsides to implementing the principles and practices of the new change management in your organization?

CHAPTER 11

DESIGN WORK WITH ENGAGEMENT BUILT IN

Evidence : Gallup Q 12

→ More productive workplace

→ Increased dignity meaning & community

four Secrets...

1 Meaning matters

→ Work/significance of work

→ "Lights up" brain

→ Janitor or contributor to Education for a community ?

2 Put Autonomy In charge

→ freedom to make DECISIONS

→ reduce "red tape"

3 Construct your own SCOREBOARDS instant feedback

4 Create CHALLENGES

"just right" → x too much
→ x too little

Clear goals → enable "FLOW"
→ Eliminate distractions

Design Work with Engagement Built In

With the rush to reap the benefits of an engaged workforce, leaders often focus on improving relationships at work. This is not surprising when you look at popular engagement surveys such as the Gallup Q12. The Gallup Q12 reinforces the idea that relationships drive engagement with questions like, Do you have a best friend at work? Does your supervisor, or someone at work, seem to care about you as a person? Gallup's research shows that these are important considerations. And while other elements of the Q12 measure the opportunity to learn and grow and the need for clear expectations, they merely give a nod to work redesign (Thackray 2001).

WORK DESIGNED WITH ENGAGEMENT BUILT IN LEADS TO A PRODUCTIVE WORKPLACE

Creating an engaged workplace requires more than productive relationships. Jobs must have engagement in their DNA. This is not an either-or proposition. You need both. My point is that work design is engagement's stepchild.

Organizations put great thought into designing organizations so everything runs smoothly and the organization can effectively respond to turbulent environments. However, other than creating the job descriptions necessary to determine pay scales, organizational designers rarely give thought to the work itself.

I learned firsthand the benefits of work design when I was working for General Foods. At the time, General Foods' approach to employee participation was one of the most innovative in the United States. In building the Topeka plant, General Foods not only built a new facility, they built a new way of working. The design of work and the organizational structure at the Topeka plant facilitated what we would now call "engagement." I saw how engaged people became when they learned and grew on the job while taking on new responsibilities. Productivity soared. Topeka was always one of the most productive plants in the General Foods organization.

As the organization development manager in Chicago, I was responsible for taking the insights from Topeka and applying them to organizations that had existed for more than thirty years. Again, the results were the same. In fact, one organization was so productive that no one could believe the results. So the corporate auditors made frequent visits to Chicago to make sure we weren't "cooking the books."

EVEN MATURE ORGANIZATIONS CAN DESIGN FOR ENGAGEMENT

"We were like a refugee camp. We worked for the same company but spoke different languages. Shock resulting from a downturn in our industry permeated everyone. We were confused and without organizational homes. Survival meant creating a new way of life," explains Mike Freeman, former director of Hewlett-Packard's MicroElectronics Operation. "The challenges were enormous. We had five different organizations, we were located on one site, and we had to transform ourselves into an integrated manufacturing organization in the face of a changing and uncertain market" (M. Freeman, pers. comm., August 26, 1999).

Mike and his leadership team decided to create a workplace with jobs designed with engagement in mind. Using the Conference Model, they successfully engaged the organization and converted this refugee camp into an efficient, collaborative, customer-focused organization that has recorded productivity improvements of 18 percent each year for the last five years.

Work redesign at the federal courts enabled staff to increase the volume of work while reducing costs. One court returned nearly $1 million from its budget to the government in a gain-sharing arrangement that also allowed the court to distribute part of the gain back to the staff as a bonus. Court staff used Emery and Trist's design criteria to design their work (Rehm 2000):

- Variety and challenge
- Elbow room for decision making
- Feedback and learning
- Mutual support and respect
- Wholeness and meaning
- Room to grow (Emery and Trist 1960)

FOUR SECRETS OF CREATING ENGAGING WORK

It's not hard to design work with engagement in mind. Here are four secrets that are secrets no more.

Secret 1: Find Meaning

Meaning can come from the work itself or from the significance you attach to the work. For example, meaning for healthcare professionals and teachers can come from knowing that they contribute to the greater good of society. Remember our lesson from neuroscience that contributing to the greater good increases a person's status, which in turn lights up the innovative, creative, collaborative brain.

Not everyone's job has meaning built in. The janitor who takes pride in the cleanliness of his rooms, the gurney driver who treats her patients as if they were riding in her private limousine, and the grill cook who keeps an immaculate grill have all found ways to find meaning in what they do. For example, if you are a janitor in a school, you might see your work as contributing to educating children. Companies like Timberland and Cirque du Soleil help people find meaning because they provide people avenues to serve their communities. Or, most importantly, you may gain meaning because of the contribution your work makes to your family's well-being.

The work itself may contain meaning, or people may find meaning in the work they do. In either case, as meaning increases, so does engagement.

Secret 2: Put Autonomy in Charge

Autonomy is the ability to make decisions on your own without having to go through endless red tape. Remember Chris at Best Buy? One of the reasons she loves working at Best Buy is her freedom to make appropriate decisions in her job. Research by Hackman and Oldham (1976) shows that when people have autonomy in their work, the job's motivating potential improves, which in turn impacts productivity and customer service. One of the great benefits of self-directed work teams is that individuals and teams take on decisions that supervisors would have made. This in turn frees up supervisors to actually lead.

Secret 3: Construct Your Own Scoreboards

Scoreboards provide instant feedback. At a glance, you know whether you are ahead or behind and how much time remains in the game. Scoreboards are neutral feedback devices. They just provide the facts. They don't add value judgments. Talking heads do that.

When I refer to feedback, I'm not talking about what you hear from your boss during a performance review. While that information is important, it cannot have the impact of immediate feedback that regularly lets you know how well you are doing. Your computer's spell-checker is an everyday feedback example. Your spell-checker lets you know immediately when you've made a spelling error. It does not call you "stupid." It just lets you know. The readability statistics available in most word processors provide information about word counts, readability, and your writing's grade level. This readily available information allows you to adjust your writing on the spot.

One of the great appeals of video games is that you know instantly how well you are doing. In addition, the memory function lets you measure progress over time. The thermometer chart in the village square that shows contributions to the community chest drive lets the community see its progress. Corporate dashboards, with their red light/yellow light/green light symbols, provide a similar function.

TABLE 11.1

FOUR SECRETS FROM FOUR PERSPECTIVES

Secret	1960s–1970s Emery and Trist's job design criteria	1970s–1980s Hackman and Oldham's work redesign	1990s Csikszent- mihalyi's flow	2009 Rock's SCARF model
Meaning matters	Jobs where you can complete a whole task from beginning to end provide meaning to individuals.	Meaning comes from the work itself.	Work provides meaning. People invest meaning in their work.	Status increases when you derive personal meaning from your work or what the organization does or provides to the world.
Put autonomy in charge	The scope of decision making needs to be increased.	Freedom, independence, and discretion need to be increased.	People need to take owner- ship for their own actions.	Autonomy increases when you are able to take action.
Construct your own score- boards	Opportunities for feedback and learning need to be built into the job.	Work activities provide direct and clear feed- back about your performance.	Immediate feedback creates the optimal experience.	Certainty increases when you get feedback. Fair- ness increases when the feed- back comes from a neutral source.
Create challenges	Learning new skills and doing different tasks creates chal- lenge.	Jobs that re- quire learning new skills and doing different tasks create challenge.	Tasks slightly above your current skill level produce engagement. Goals focus attention.	Status increases when you successfully meet a challenge.

Secret 4: Create Challenges

Challenge is like Goldilocks's porridge: you need to get it just right. Too much challenge makes people give up. Not enough challenge makes people say, "Why bother?" In his book *Finding Flow*, Mihaly Csikszentmihalyi (1997) says that a challenge slightly above your skill level engages you. Whether it is getting to the next level of your video game, learning how to use a computer program, or figuring out how to do your work better, challenge engages.

My wife, Emily, is fond of reminding me about the day it took me eight hours to fix an electrical problem in our house. We have an old house. If you have ever lived in an old house, you know that repairs are never simple. What kept me engaged for eight hours? The challenge of figuring out the wiring without circuit diagrams so that electricity was actually there when you flipped the switch.

Everyone understands the importance of clear goals. But Csikszentmihalyi provides an interesting twist when it comes to goals: "It helps to have clear goals, not because achieving goals is so important but because without clear goals it is difficult to concentrate and avoid distraction" (ibid., 137). Engaged people are not easily distracted.

Table 11.1 summarizes the four secrets that are not so secret anymore.

You may think that human resource professionals or other social architects do work design best. Not true. The best results occur when people doing the job design their own work. The questions in table 11.2 provide a guide for you to use if you decide to move toward jobholder-designed work.

TABLE 11.2

QUESTIONS WHOSE ANSWERS LEAD TO ENGAGING WORK

How much variety do I currently experience in my work?	How much variety do I want to experience in my work?
How much autonomy do I currently experience in my work?	How much autonomy do I want to experience?
How much meaning do I currently experience in my work?	How much meaning do I want to experience?
How much challenge do I currently experience in my work?	How much challenge do I want to experience?
How much room to grow do I currently experience in my work?	How much room to grow do I want to experience?
How much feedback do I currently experience in my work?	How much feedback do I want to experience?
How much respect and support do I currently experience in my work?	How much respect and support do I want to experience?

In *Productive Workplaces*, Marvin Weisbord writes, "The quickest way to increase dignity, meaning, and community in a workplace is to involve people in redesigning their own work. That is also the shortest route—in the long run—to lower costs, higher quality, and more satisfied customers" (Weisbord 1987, 311).

KEY POINTS

▷ Work design is engagement's stepchild.

▷ Design work with engagement built in.

▷ Meaning, autonomy, feedback, and challenge are the keys to the four secrets of designing engaging work.

▷ Bonus secret: Involving people in the design of their own work is more effective than designing work for them.

QUESTIONS FOR REFLECTION

▷ How can we introduce new and interesting tasks into the work we do?

▷ How can we increase the freedom to make decisions on our own into the work we do?

▷ How can we introduce mechanisms that allow people to know how they are performing into the work we do?

▷ How can we build challenge into the work we do?

How to
Start where you are

1 Start with yourself
- → what you **DO** is more important than what you say
- → practice engaging conversations → Listening → Straight talking
- → take meetings seriously
- → dialogue with your team

2 Start with a key business issue
- ⤷ needs attention

3 Start with a change process already underway
- ⤷ do an assessment
- → look at the four engagement principles

4 Start by redesigning work
- → ask questions
- → clear goals & challenges
- → assess team effectiveness

FARM case-study
metaphor
- → till the soil
- → plant a few seeds
- → weed the garden
- → water the plants
- → reap the harvest

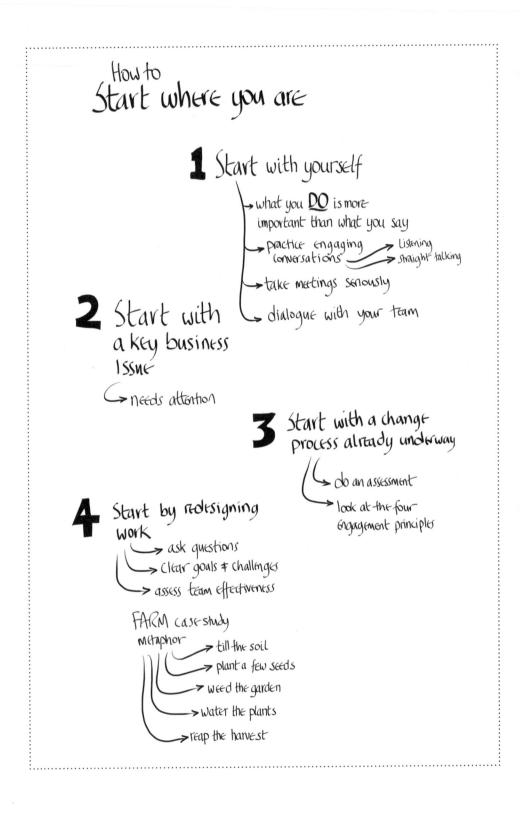

CHAPTER 12

How to Start
Where You Are

No matter how you have read this book, my wish is that the principles, practices, and stories in *Terms of Engagement* have inspired you to take action. If they didn't, read no further and enjoy the rest of your day! If you are inspired, here are four suggestions about where and how to start.

- You can start with yourself.
- You can start with a key business issue whose success requires an engaged organization.
- You can start with a change process already underway.
- You can start by redesigning work.

There is no right place to start. Just pick one.

START WITH YOURSELF

Whether you are a CEO or a supervisor, the place to start is with yourself. Engagement is contagious. If you are engaged in what you are doing, people pick up your excitement and will want to join you. I'm not talking about cheerleading. I'm talking about the contagious excitement that comes when you really believe in what you are doing.

The question to ask is, Why are you are personally willing to put your own time and energy behind what needs to be done? If you find yourself saying that it's to improve profits or provide better customer service, you are taking the easy way out. Remember the teacher in chapter 7 who wanted to create a safe school? The engagement that came from wanting to create a safe school is very different from the management goal of improving test scores. Once you can say why you are personally willing to put time and energy into what you are asking others to do, you are ready to engage others.

Practice Engaging Conversations

In chapter 4, we learned the importance of honesty, transparency, and trust. Trying to tackle all three at once is probably too much. Pick one to work on. Ask yourself, How can I increase my current level of honesty? What information can I share that will lead to increased transparency? Or, What can I do to build trust on a daily basis? Remember, when a crisis hits, it's too late to build trust. Here are some practices to help you.

- *Find out what people in your organization care about.* It takes only a few minutes to learn what is important to the people who work with you. Work is what brings us all together in the first place. Asking strengthens relationships.

- *Let people know what you care about and why.* When you speak from the heart, it makes a difference.

- *Take time for appreciation.* It takes only a minute to say thank you or to recognize someone's effort or contribution.

- *Treat employees' goals as if they were your own.* Whether people desire to learn and grow on the job, have more autonomy, or even get the next promotion, engagement grows when they know you are there to support them in what they are doing.

- *Start slowly.* You need to build your engagement muscle. Try one conversation a day and limit it to fifteen minutes. Use the six attentive listening skills outlined in chapter 10. As your engagement muscle builds, you will be ready and able to do more.

- *Practice.* Practice is the defining characteristic of greatness. Athletes, musicians, and artists, no matter how talented, put in many practice hours. Michael Jordan was always the last to leave practice. His work effort during practice produced greatness.

Take Meetings Seriously

Meetings are the most important fast-track engagement opportunity available. Every boring, time-wasting meeting you conduct saps energy, fostering disengagement. Decide which meetings you conduct are necessary. Make sure that the right people are present. By the right people, I mean those who have information, those who are responsible for the outcomes, those who can make decisions, and those affected by the outcomes. And yes, don't forget those who opposed you at first. They will make your meeting more interesting while adding valuable insights.

Develop a process for soliciting agenda items from participants. Use the meeting canoe to design your meeting. Save time at the end of your meetings to review what worked, what didn't work, and how you can make your next meeting better. If you take these actions regularly, you will be happy with the results.

Dialogue with Your Team

Create your own "Engagement University" by setting aside time to discuss the key points and questions for reflection at the end of each chapter. Remember to strive for understanding first and agreement second. I've provided a quick summary of each chapter's key points and discussion questions after this chapter as a guide.

Leaders listen. Practice leadership conversations by dialoguing with your team about a current issue facing your team. Use the following framework, which I developed to enhance leadership conversations. Discussing these questions, which are based on Peter Koestenbaum's Leadership Diamond, will give you new insights and lead you to new actions. You don't have to use all the questions. Pick one or two from each category that fit your situation.

Reality questions:

- What are the facts?
- How did you come to that conclusion?
- What events contributed to this situation?
- What are you seeing or hearing?
- What obstacles are present?
- What is the bottom line?

Vision questions:

- What do you want to create?
- What will it look like if you are successful?
- How could you imagine work being different?
- What is the long view?
- What are your dreams?

Ethics questions:

- What does it mean to be a decent person in this situation?
- What is the likely impact on others?
- What is the right thing to do?
- How might people see what you are doing as unscrupulous?
- What would you do if no one were looking?
- What is the negative impact on people of your work?
- What might be the unintended consequences of your work?

Courage questions:

- What will success require of you?
- What do you need to do that you have been avoiding?
- What do you need to say that you have been avoiding?
- What are you afraid of?
- Whose support do you need to be courageous?
- What crossroads are you at? Which path will you follow?
- What is your truth?

START WITH A KEY BUSINESS ISSUE

Connecting engagement with a key business issue is critical because it brings reality to your work. Here are eight factors to keep in mind.

1. Identify an issue that needs attention. Use the previously identified Leadership Diamond questions to assess the situation with your team. Start with the reality questions. Then discuss the vision questions. Move to the ethics questions.

Conclude with the courage questions. By the time you finish, you'll know what to do.

2. Compare the principles and practices of the new change management with your current way of introducing change in your organization. Discuss the upside and downside of each with your team. Decide if the principles and practices of the new change management are right for you.

3. No matter what change process you use, create a compelling purpose. Ask and answer Kathy Dannemiller's question: What will be different in the world because this group of people came together to do this work? Follow up by asking and answering the questions, To what end? In order to do what? You'll know your purpose is compelling when there is excitement in the room.

4. Use the four engagement principles as your guide: widen the circle of involvement, connect people to each other, create communities for action, and promote fairness. Gary Short, director of HR global projects for Kimberly-Clark Corporation, says it best: "You can overcome tactical errors; you can't overcome errors in principles" (G. Short, pers. comm., August 12, 2009).

5. Create freedom within frameworks. Be clear about what is open for discussion and what isn't. Good frameworks provide a safe place to play. If there is too much room, people flounder. If there is not enough, people say, "Why bother?"

6. Identify key stakeholders:
   - People with information, authority, responsibility
   - People who care about the issue
   - People who are opposed to what you do
   - People from different levels and functions
   - External stakeholders such as customers and suppliers

7. Form a design team to develop processes for engaging the organization in the task. This group, representing a microcosm of the organization:
   - Deepens the initial purpose
   - Identifies stakeholders
   - Designs the engagement process
   - Ensures timely and open communication
   - Plans for implementation

   Remember that the role of the design team is not to solve the issue at hand; rather, it is to design the process for engaging the organization in creating a new future.
8. Find any engagement gaps created by a lack of voice, isolation, fear, and a lack of trust in leaders and the organization. Use walkthrus to monitor whether these gaps are increasing or decreasing throughout the change process. Work hard to minimize these gaps.

START WITH AN ONGOING CHANGE PROCESS

If you have a change process already underway, you can do an assessment. Check out the current state of your engagement gaps. Depending on what you find, you may want to take drastic action like Detroit Edison and essentially start over, following steps one through seven in the previous section. If you choose to start over, be sure to figure out—as Detroit Edison did—how to preserve the good work done to date while you follow the principles and practices of the new change management.

If you decide not to take drastic action, look at the four engagement principles:

1. See how wide your circle is and determine who else needs to be included.

2. See which of the four connectors needs strengthening. Is it shared experience, relationships, purpose, or storytelling?

3. See which of the keys to community you need to use to unlock your organization's spirit: creating a compelling purpose, putting people at the center, valuing differences, encouraging dialogue, unleashing talent, committing to the communities where you work, or giving back.

4. Promote fairness by increasing information sharing, involving people in decisions that affect them, increasing autonomy, and listening as if your life depended on it. Remember, fairness pays.

START BY REDESIGNING WORK

Work is what we do every day. It can be the source of great frustration or immense satisfaction. Discuss the questions at the end of chapter 11 either individually or collectively with your group. Together, redesign the work based on the responses you receive.

Provide clear goals and challenge. All the while, ensure that the challenges you provide are slightly above the current skill level of the people you are challenging.

If you call yourself a team, make sure you are a team. Check your group against Hackman's (1990) criteria for effective teams from *Groups That Work (and Those That Don't)*:

1. Is the group's task clear and consistent with the group's purpose?

2. Does the group have meaningful work to do?

3. Is the group sized right to accomplish its task?

4. Do team members have the right skills and expertise?

5. Do team members have sufficient interpersonal skills?

6. Does the group have enough similarities and differences so it functions?

7. Do group norms support effective performance?

FRASER HEALTH—HOW A BAND OF SISTERS CHANGED THE CULTURE

When it comes to change, Fraser Health does it with engagement in mind. If you are a doctor, nurse, or other worker at Fraser Health, whenever change is in the air, you will be engaged. However, it wasn't always this way.

First, Till the Soil

Our work with Fraser began in an ordinary room slightly larger than a standard conference room, several mergers ago. There a dozen or so human resource professionals and OD consultants gathered for a workshop based on the first edition of *Terms of Engagement*. Little did we know we were tilling the soil for a significant cultural change. Hugh MacLeod, then vice president of the South Fraser Health Authority, was to call this workshop the most powerful educational experience of his career.

Organizational change folklore states that success requires leadership from the top. Leaders create the vision and then forge buy-in by selling their vision of the organization. The Fraser story is not about a change process whose half-life is the current CEO's tenure. This is the story of a guerrilla change led by a small but significant group of women who, with great will, determination, and belief in the new change management's principles and practices, shifted Fraser Health Authority's culture.

In case you were thinking that Fraser Health is a small mom-and-pop operation, let me tell you a bit about the organization. Located on the lower mainland of British Columbia, Fraser Health is responsible for the delivery of all publicly funded acute and community health-care services for 1.5 million people from Burnaby to White Rock to Hope in British Columbia. In practical terms, this means delivering everything from public health initiatives like immunizations to end-of-life services like hospice. The Fraser Health service area is the largest and fastest-growing health-care region in Canada. Fraser works within an annual budget of more than $2 billion, with 23,000 employees and 2,300 physicians (Fraser Health n.d.).

Plant a Few Seeds

Over the years, we have trained OD consultants, HR professionals, project management specialists, quality assurance specialists, and leaders at all levels in what the folks at Fraser affectionately call "Conferencing." This includes people like Geoffrey Crampton, the current vice president of Fraser Health, who always asks, "What is our engagement strategy?" whenever significant change is on the drawing board.

These trainings built their capacity to apply the new change management without becoming dependent on outside resources. At Fraser, the Collaborative Loops process was born. As you may recall, the Collaborative Loops process brings together different steering committees from around the organization to simultaneously design high-engagement change processes (Holman, Devane, and Cady 2007). In these workshops, leaders learned firsthand how to engage people in change. Today we act mostly as advisors to the staff at Fraser, serving as a sounding board for their good judgment.

Back to our band of sisters, Susan Good, Helen Lingham, Erica Groschler, Pam Theriault, and Gabi Cuff. They are extraordinary in their ability to understand what is going on in the organization and then figure out a way to apply Conferencing to the situation. This does not mean they see Conferencing as a universal tool. They are very strategic. They first seek to understand the needs of the organization and then determine if Conferencing is a good fit. They work quietly behind the scenes, with leaders helping them to grasp the opportunities and reap the rewards engagement can bring. Because their work has such a high success rate, leaders and employees expect, even require, that engagement be the cornerstone of any significant change at Fraser Health.

Weed the Garden

They are also good at saying no. Early on, an executive team asked our band of sisters to form a steering committee to lead a high-engagement change process. It was apparent to the sisters and the steering team that the executives already had the solution in mind. The leaders wanted people to feel as if they were engaged as opposed to really being engaged. So the team said thanks, but no thanks. They actually refused to do the work. You might expect the next step would be a reprimand or termination. Neither happened. Having taken a stand for principle-based change, they removed a toxic weed and made room for future success.

Provide Water to Help Your Garden Grow

Our band of sisters receives significant support from senior leadership. In addition to Geoff Crampton always asking the engagement question, you have Dr. Nigel Murray, president and CEO of Fraser Health Authority, who not only asks the engagement question but also conducts a quarterly business meeting with 350 of the organization's leaders. This is not your typical "sit and get" leadership briefing. These voluntary meetings, based on the engagement principles and designed using the meeting canoe, have a loyal and growing following. Expected attendance at the most recent meeting was 350 people; 500 showed up.

Reap the Harvest

Here are a few examples of successful initiatives at Fraser in the past ten years:

- Teams across Fraser Health reduced the time it took to complete the hospital accreditation self-assessment process from six months to a matter of weeks. Accreditation is a bugaboo at any hospital.

- At Fraser Health's Langley Hospital, people came together to figure out how to help long-term-care patients become more independent. This process was so successful that Langley decided to implement projects in the maternity unit, licensed practical nurse interface, registered nurse care delivery model, and total hip replacement unit. In the hip replacement project, the length of stay for patients dropped by 33 percent.

- When it was time to build the new hospital at Abbotsford, doctors, nurses, staff, patients, and members of the community came together to create a vision for the new hospital and develop new processes for providing patient care. At the end of the conference, participants identified and volunteered to work on seventeen projects that would advance "extraordinary care and service." For example, one group volunteered to videotape patients talking about their hospital experiences. These videos would then be used to educate hospital staff. Another group decided to work on making the atrium a community gathering place. A year after the move into the new building, people came together for a series of "Now What? Conferences," where people who had volunteered to work on projects shared their successes.

- Remember the Gallup surveys that measure employee engagement? Fraser used Conferencing to bring teams of people together, review the survey results, and develop plans for the future. The leaders at Fraser do not believe in thermometer solutions, where leaders read the results and decide what to do. They engage with the people who filled out the survey in the first place and together they decide what needs attention.

- The most recent major change initiative, transitioning from site-based management to program-based management, affects almost every job in Fraser Health. Instead of each hospital having its own surgery department, one surgery department cuts across all the hospitals in Fraser Health. Instead of people being told how the system will work, people are coming together in dozens of one-day conferences to create a new way of delivering health care. These conferences are designed with an engagement edge.

- The work at Fraser is spreading throughout British Columbia. When other health authorities face significant change, they often contact Fraser to find out how the situation was handled there.

Gardening Advice

Recently I spoke with Helen Lingham and Susan Good, who initiated Conferencing at Fraser. It was Helen Lingham who first contacted me. Neither of us will forget our first phone call. It ended with my saying that what she was requesting was overscoped and underresourced. I didn't hear from Helen for a while, but when she called again we started with the introductory workshop described at the beginning of this story. We haven't looked back since. Here are their lessons learned, in Susan's and Helen's voices:

> We started out thinking this was a kinder, gentler way to get people to deal with resistance. It is much more powerful. Engagement shifts the culture at the level of belief.
>
> With engagement, people move from believing they don't have a voice to believing their voice counts. They start out believing what they say doesn't matter. In the end, they believe they know what needs to happen. They can move something they care about forward.
>
> In the beginning, we were more structured. We followed the Conference Model as you use a recipe, step by step. Even though we were doing good work in smaller settings, we didn't think it counted unless we had several hundred people in the room. Now we just ask, "What conversations need to happen? Who needs to be involved in these

conversations? What is the best way to convene people for these conversations?"

Engagement does not require a senior executive doing a selling job on the organization. You start where people are. You look at what is going on in the organization and where engagement would make a difference. Is there a meeting where people are disengaged? Is there a project where new and different voices would make a difference? You use engagement to provide people with a different kind of experience. The shift is from being a passive recipient to becoming an active player in your own experience. After a while, it begins to take on a life of its own. Now it's just the way we go about change around here.

Now that's the legacy of the work that you and Emily initiated us into. Isn't it amazing? (Good and Lingham, pers. comm., February 16, 2010)

THE BALL IS NOW IN YOUR COURT

So now you have it, *Terms of Engagement*. I have given principles to guide you, practices to sharpen your skills, and stories to inspire you. Now success is up to you.

KEY POINTS

▷ You can start anywhere.

▷ You can start by examining your own leadership style.

▷ You can start with a key business issue that needs attention.

▷ You can start with a change process already underway.

▷ You can start by redesigning work with engagement in mind.

▷ Be a good farmer; till the soil, plant a few seeds, weed the garden, water the plants, reap the harvest.

QUESTIONS FOR REFLECTION

▷ Where do you want to start?

▷ How do you want to start?

▷ What concerns you most about starting?

▷ What is your motivation for starting?

▷ If you decide to move forward, whose help and support do you need?

Chapter Reviews

What follows is a quick summary of each chapter's key points and questions for reflection.

CHAPTER 1. WHY CHANGE MANAGEMENT NEEDS CHANGING

Key Points

- The old change management works against innovation and creativity.
- When people do not have a voice in change that affects them, they will resist even if the change benefits them.
- Engagement gaps increase when
  - You believe that your voice does not count.
  - You are isolated from key people, events, and processes.
  - You are fearful.
  - You don't trust the institution and its leaders.

Questions for Reflection

- What are your own beliefs about organizational change?
- To what extent do a lack of voice, isolation, fear, and low trust exist in your organization? What are the causes?

- What are the upsides and downsides for you and your organization to continue using the old change management?

CHAPTER 2. ENGAGEMENT IS THE NEW CHANGE MANAGEMENT

Key Points

- The four engagement principles—widen the circle of involvement, connect people to each other, create communities for action, and promote fairness—provide direction for engaging your organization.
- The three key practices—honesty, transparency, and trust—are the basis of any successful change process.
- The new change management increases status, certainty, autonomy, relatedness, and fairness, which in turn lights up the creative parts of the brain.

Questions for Reflection

- What are the upsides and downsides for you and your organization to use the new change management as the basis for your next change initiative?
- How do the lessons from the Detroit Edison and Calgary Health Region stories apply to you and your organization today?
- How can you build status, certainty, autonomy, relatedness, and fairness into what you do?
- What will the new change management require of you as a leader?

CHAPTER 3. SIX CHANGE MANAGEMENT MYTHS

Key Points

- Myths are just myths.
- Confronting myths leads to success.
- Leading the new change management requires a shift in roles.
- The new change management is not risk free.

Questions for Reflection

- Which of the six myths in this chapter do you believe the most?
- What would change if you no longer believed that myth?
- How are you prepared to shift your role?
- In adopting the new change management, what risks are you willing to take?
- What risks are you not willing to take?

CHAPTER 4. LEAD WITH AN ENGAGEMENT EDGE

Key Points

- Everyone makes the choice about whether or not to engage.
- Trust involves choices.
- The honesty expectation creates safety.
- Transparency provides the information necessary for people to make choices.
- Trust builds through multiple conversations.
- Integrity, the power of keeping your word, has bottom-line implications.

Questions for Reflection

- Think of a current situation where you would like to engage others. What is your goal? What would you like to be different?
- What kind of relationship do you currently have with people you would like to engage? What kind of relationship do you want to have?
- What will you need to stop, start, or continue to do to engage?
- What will success require of you?

CHAPTER 5. LEADERSHIP CONVERSATIONS THAT FOSTER ENGAGEMENT

Key Points

- People resent not having a voice in changes that affect them, even if the result will benefit them.
- Everyday interactions are the basis for engagement.
- Find out what people care about by asking them what they care about at work and why.
- Support others in achieving their goals.
- Share what you care about by letting others know why you are willing to put your own time and energy behind an initiative.
- Meetings are the most overlooked fast-track engagement opportunity available.

Questions for Reflection

- To what extent do people's voices count in your organization?
- Do you know what is important to people in your organization?

- What would it mean if you treated employee goals as your own?
- To what extent do you share with the people in your organization why you personally care about a change initiative?
- What would you do differently if you treated everyday meetings as engagement opportunities?

CHAPTER 6. WIDEN THE CIRCLE OF INVOLVEMENT

Key Points

- People support what they have a hand in creating. Eric Trist said, "Unless we invent ways for large numbers of people to experience paradigm shifts, then change will remain a myth" (Weisbord and Janoff, 2000, 22).
- The belief that you can create all the vital changes by yourself is a barrier to widening the circle.
- Widening the circle produces many champions.
- New ideas grow when people with different points of view interact.
- Learning occurs when you continually inquire about what is working and what is not working.
- Widening the circle accelerates the ability to respond to turbulent environments.

Questions for Reflection

- Who else needs to be included? Whose voice is required?
- How will you introduce variety into your change process?
- What are you doing to support organizational learning?
- What innovative ways can you develop to widen the circle of involvement?
- How wide should your circle be?

CHAPTER 7. CONNECT PEOPLE TO EACH OTHER

Key Points

- Unless you are able to connect people to the task and with each other, nothing happens.
- The first connector is shared experience.
- The second connector is relationships.
- The third connector is purpose.
- The fourth connector is storytelling.

Questions for Reflection

- What is the story of your organization?
- What was your experience your first day at work in this organization?
- To what extent do you feel connected to your organization's purpose?
- What is the current state of relationships in your organization?
- How can you go about creating shared experiences in your organization?

CHAPTER 8. CREATE COMMUNITIES FOR ACTION

Key Points

- Community allows you to do together what you cannot do alone.
- "A vibrant community [is one] where talented people are loyal to one another and their collective work, everyone feels that they are part of something extraordinary" (Mintzberg 2009).

- Remember the seven strategies for creating conditions where community can thrive:
  1. Create a compelling purpose.
  2. Put people at the center.
  3. Value differences.
  4. Encourage dialogue.
  5. Unleash talent.
  6. Commit to the communities where you work.
  7. Give back.
- Boundaries create freedom.

Questions for Reflection

- How many communities do you belong to?
- What defines these communities?
- What makes them work?
- What workplace communities need attention?
- What will increasing community at work require of you?

CHAPTER 9. PROMOTE FAIRNESS

Key Points

- Ignoring fairness is a risky proposition.
- Ask the process fairness question: Are the methods used fair?
- Ask the results fairness question: Is the outcome fair?
- Ask the transactional fairness question: Does fairness exist as you implement policies and procedures?
- Apply the fairness test to decision making and information sharing.
- Increasing autonomy increases fairness.
- Trust people to make fair decisions for the good of the whole.

Questions for Reflection

- Are the methods you use fair?
- Do these methods result in fair outcomes?
- Do people experience fairness in your organization?
- Does fairness play a part in information sharing, decision making, and providing autonomy?

CHAPTER 10. WHEN ENGAGEMENT DISENGAGES: SOME WORDS OF CAUTION BEFORE YOU BEGIN

Key Points

- When the new change management goes wrong, you are actually worse off than if you never started.
- When self-deception occurs, disengagement follows.
- Straight talk and attentive listening are the antidotes to disengagement.
- Beware of these threats to the change process:
  1. Different rules for different folks
  2. Disengaging conversations
  3. I count/you don't count behaviors
  4. Past organizational damage
  5. Thermometer solutions
  6. Loss of will
  7. Collective folly
  8. The impulse to manipulate
  9. The new change management's shadow
- Even the new change management has its own downsides

Questions for Reflection

- Where does self-deception live in your organization?
- How are you sabotaging your own efforts to engage the organization?
- What could you do to ensure that your current change initiatives fail?
- When and where can you start practicing straight talk and attentive listening?
- What are the upsides and downsides to implementing the principles and practices of the new change management in your organization?

CHAPTER 11. DESIGN WORK WITH ENGAGEMENT BUILT IN

Key Points

- Work design is engagement's stepchild.
- Design work with engagement built in.
- Meaning, autonomy, feedback, and challenge are the keys to the four secrets of designing engaging work.
- Bonus secret: Involving people in the design of their own work is more effective than designing work for them.

Questions for Reflection

- How can we introduce new and interesting tasks into the work we do?
- How can we increase the freedom to make decisions on our own into the work we do?
- How can we introduce mechanisms that allow people to know how they are performing into the work we do?
- How can we build challenge into the work we do?

CHAPTER 12. HOW TO START WHERE YOU ARE

Key Points

- You can start anywhere.

- You can start by examining your own leadership style.

- You can start with a key business issue that needs attention.

- You can start with a change process already underway.

- You can start by redesigning work with engagement in mind.

- Be a good farmer; till the soil, plant a few seeds, weed the garden, water the plants, reap the harvest.

Questions for Reflection

- Where do you want to start?

- How do you want to start?

- What concerns you most about starting?

- What is your motivation for starting?

- If you decide to move forward, whose help and support do you need?

RESORCES

For many people, how to build trust is a mystery. Here are some useful ways to think about trust.

HOW TO BUILD TRUST

- Everyone knows what it's like to trust, to be trusted, and to be wary of trusting—but when it comes to understanding exactly what defines trust, it often seems difficult to grasp. Dennis and Michelle Reina, authors of *Trust and Betrayal in the Workplace*, provide helpful guidance for identifying trust's components. They identify three elements of transactional trust:

- Competence Trust, the trust of capabilities

- Communication Trust, the trust of disclosure

- Contractual Trust, the trust of character

Competence Trust allows individuals to leverage and further develop skills, abilities, and knowledge. The Chiefs Program at West Monroe Partners exhibits competence trust when people follow their interests to improve the organization.

Communication Trust establishes information flow and how people talk with each other. Henri Lipmanowicz and Carla Zuniga talked about Communication Trust when they shared the importance they placed on free-flowing information.

Contractual Trust sets the tone for engagement and direction, and shapes roles and responsibilities. When Carla Zuniga talked about managing commitments and keeping one's word, she was talking about contractual trust.

The Reinas sum up the importance of trust when they say, "Without trust, employees have little interest in being creative, taking risks, and being collaborative" (Reina and Reina 2007, 36).

John Carter, a faculty member at the Gestalt Institute in Cleveland, Ohio, has developed a model for thinking about trust that is useful for those leaders who do not wish to run the risk of violating the trust of their organization (see figure R.1). He calls it the "Trust Triangle."

The foundation of the triangle is *straight talk*. Straight talk means sharing all of the information available in an honest and forthright manner. It does not mean doling out partial truths or sharing only the information that supports a point of view or course of action. It means providing all of the available facts, your thoughts and feelings about those facts, and what you would like to have happen.

Straight talk must partner with *listening for understanding*. When we listen for understanding, not only do we gain more information, but others trust us more. For more on this idea, you can read about attentive listening in chapter 10, in the section titled "Threat 2: Disengaging Conversations."

The next component of the triangle is *making commitments*. When we make a commitment, we are pledging ourselves to a course of action. We build trust by keeping our commitments.

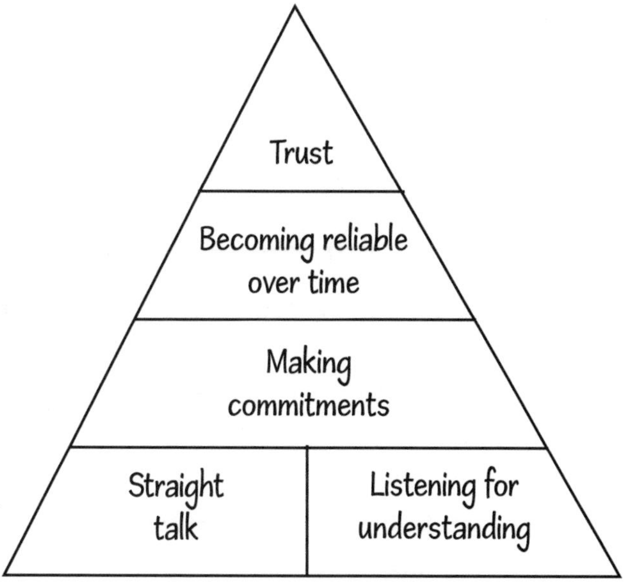

Figure R.1

Trust triangle

(adapted from John Carter's Trust Triangle in an unpublished paper by Howard K. Jackson and John D. Carter, Gestalt OSD Center, 2000)

Sometimes we make commitments we cannot keep. Leaders embarrassed by this fact usually fail to say or do anything about it, hoping that it will just go away, instead of dealing with the issue directly. When commitments simply disappear, trust is broken. To avoid this outcome, leaders must use straight talk to explain what happened and why they cannot keep their commitments, made in good faith.

The next component of trust is *becoming reliable over time.* This means doing what you say you are going to do. It means that you are true to your word and that people can count on you. This is an extension of making commitments. When organization members can put faith in their leaders to both make and keep commitments, these leaders become reliable over time.

When leaders engage in straight talk, listen for understanding, make commitments, and become reliable over time, they become trustworthy and are able to engage the organization in change.

A BRIEF HISTORY OF THE NEW CHANGE MANAGEMENT

In the early 1990s, we (the Axelrod Group) helped pioneer using large group interventions to change organizations when we created the Conference Model. (Axelrod and Axelrod 1999). The Conference Model is recognized as part of the original group of interventions that have revolutionized the practice of organizational change. Other interventions include

- The Future Search Conference—a process by which diverse groups discover common futures (Weisbord and Janoff 1995)

- Real Time Strategic Change—a process for aligning and creating collective futures while developing new strategies and directions (Jacobs 1994)

- Whole Scale Change—a process for connecting an organization so that it has one brain and one heart (Dannemiller Tyson Associates 2000)

- Open Space Technologies—a process in which people self-organize around what they really care about to get things done (Owen 2008)

- Appreciative Inquiry Summit—a strength-based process for improving organizations (Ludema, et al. 2003)

- America Speaks—a process for conducting town meetings on public policy issues (Lukensmeyer and Jacobson 2007)

- World Café—a process for hosting conversations about questions that matter (Brown and Isaacs 2005)

Since large group interventions first came on the scene, many others have added to the library of knowledge. Three excellent resources for further reading are *Large Group Interventions: Engaging the Whole System for Rapid Change* (Bunker and Alban 1997), *The Handbook of Large Group Methods: Creating Systemic Change in Organizations and Communities* (Bunker and Alban 2006), and *The Change Handbook: The Definitive Resource on Today's Best Methods for Engaging Whole Systems* (Holman, Devane, and Cady 2007).

The new change management's four core principles provide a way to understand what is going on in these interventions, as well as a guide for creating and implementing new interventions. These large group interventions brought the whole system into the room for the first time to address systemic issues. These interventions were a significant break from the waterfall change processes that were common at the time.

The Conference Model has two unique features. First, it consists of a series of connected conferences that are held every four to six weeks. This series of linked conferences creates organizational momentum and allows issues to be addressed at increasing levels of depth. "Walkthrus," the second unique feature, are miniconferences held for those organization members who are not able to attend the main conferences. In these miniconferences, participants are informed by a communications team, which we call the "data assist team," of the results of the large group sessions and are invited to provide input into the change process. Thus, they receive feedback on what has happened to date and their input is incorporated into the proceedings prior to the next session. Walkthrus are more than briefings; in fact, they have the look and feel of the large group sessions.

How the New Change Management Turns the Old Change Management on Its Head

Together, the combination of integrated conferences and walk-thrus turns the current change management paradigm on its head. Instead of small groups determining what needs to be changed and then selling it to the rest of the organization, a critical mass of the organization comes together to identify the future. Small groups may be needed after a conference, but their role is to add detail to what has been decided in the conferences, not to determine the nature and direction of the change process (Axelrod and Axelrod 1999).

The Conference Model has been used successfully by large global organizations and small nonprofits to redesign organizations and processes in a variety of settings, such as health care, education, manufacturing, and government. Some leaders have even created new organizational cultures to support mergers and acquisitions.

From 1996 to 2005, Dick and Emily Axelrod were faculty members, along with Meg Wheatley, Peter Block, Peter Koestenbaum, Charlotte Roberts, Cliff Bolster, John Shuster, and the late Kathy Dannemiller, in the School for Leading Change. In this school, Dick and Emily taught participant teams how to design their own large group interventions. As a result of faculty interaction and the many workshops we conducted, the four principles that are the basis for the new change management emerged. And our own thinking about how to bring about organizational change has never been the same.

As a result, we created the Collaborative Loops process, a method for bringing people together to design their own change process. Today organizations and communities are implementing many changes simultaneously. They are improving their supply chains while installing a performance management system and incorporating lean thinking into the business. Communities are working to improve service delivery and upgrade their schools. These are not isolated events. The teams responsible for these changes need to understand how they affect one another.

Collaborative Loops brings multiple teams together in a workshop to learn how to design and implement their own change strategies based on the engagement principles. In most organizations, everyone has good intentions, but people work at cross-purposes. By bringing the network together, participants realize that they share a higher purpose: the overall success of the organization or community (Holman, Devane, and Cady 2007).

For us, the new change management is a learning experience continually updated and informed by our work with colleagues and clients.

WORKS CITED

Axelrod, Emily M., and Richard H. Axelrod. 1999. *The Conference Model*. San Francisco: Berrett-Koehler.

Axelrod, Robert, and Michael D. Cohen. 2000. *Harnessing complexity: Organizational implications of a scientific frontier*. New York: Free Press.

Bichel, Allison, Shannon Erfle, Valerie Wiebe, Dick Axelrod, and John Conly. 2009. Improving patient access to medical services: Preventing the patient from being lost in translation. *Healthcare Quarterly* 13:61–68.

Briskin, Alan, Sheryl Erickson, John Ott, and Tom Callanan. 2009. *The power of collective wisdom: And the trap of collective folly*. San Francisco: Berrett-Koehler.

Brown, Juanita, and David Isaacs. 2005. *The World Café*. San Francisco: Berrett-Koehler.

Bunker, Barbara Benedict, and Billie T. Alban. 1997. *Large group interventions: Engaging the whole system for rapid change*. San Francisco: Jossey-Bass.

———. 2006. *The handbook of large group methods: Creating systemic change in organizations and communities*. San Francisco: Jossey-Bass.

Burke, Warner. Forthcoming. On the legacy of theory Y. Special Issue, *Journal of Management History*.

Challenger, Gray & Christmas, "Hot Topics @ Work," February 10, 2010.

Coch, Lester, and John R. P. French. 1948. Overcoming resistance to change. *Human Relations* 1(4): 512–532.

Conlin, Michelle. 2009. Is optimism a competitive advantage? *Business Week*, August 24 and 31:52–53.

Conner, Daryl R. 1992. *Managing at the speed of change.* New York: Random House.

Cozzani, Charles A., and James L. Oakley. Forum for People Performance and Measurement. Executive Summary. *Incentive Performance Center.* www.incentivecentral.org/pdf/employee_engagement_study.pdf (accessed March 7, 2010).

Csikszentmihalyi, Mihaly. 1997. *Finding flow: The psychology of engagement with everyday life.* New York: HarperCollins Publishers.

Dannemiller Tyson Associates. 2000. *Whole-scale change: Unleashing the magic in organizations.* San Francisco: Berrett-Koehler.

Emery, F. E., and E. L. Trist. 1960. Socio-technical systems. In *Management Sciences, Models, and Techniques*, ed. by C. W. Churchman and others. London: Pergamon.

Fraser Health. n.d. Dr. Nigel Murray, president and CEO. http://www.fraserhealth.ca/about_us/leaership/executive_committee/dr._nigel_murray,_president_and_ceo (accessed March 15, 2010).

Fritz, Robert. 1999. *The path of least resistance for managers.* San Francisco: Berrett-Koehler.

Gallup. 2010. Employee engagement: A leading indicator of financial performance. March 7. http://www.gallup.com/consulting/52/employee-engagement.aspx (accessed March 7, 2010).

Gardner, Howard. 2006. *Changing minds: The art and science of changing our own and other people's minds.* Boston: Harvard Business School Press.

———. 1995. *Leading minds: An anatomy of leadership.* New York: Basic Books.

Gecan, Michael. 2004. *Going public: An organizer's guide to citizen action.* Garden City, NY: Anchor Books.

Hackman, J. Richard, ed. 1990. *Groups that work (and those that don't): Creating conditions for effective teamwork.* San Francisco: Jossey-Bass.

Hackman, J. R., and G. R. Oldham. 1976. Motivation through the design of work: Test of a theory. *Organizational Behavior and Human Performance* 16:250–279.

Hogan, Robert. 2007. *Personality and the fate of organizations.* Mahwah, NJ: Lawrence Erlbaum Associates.

Holman, Peggy, Tom Devane, and Steven Cady. 2007. *The change handbook: The definitive resource on today's best methods for engaging whole systems.* 2nd ed. San Francisco: Berrett-Koehler.

Jacobs, Robert W. 1994. *Real-time strategic change: How to involve an entire organization in fast and far-reaching change.* San Francisco: Berrett-Koehler Publishers.

Kim, W. Chan, and Renee Mauborgne. 2005. *Blue Ocean Strategy: How to create uncontested market space and make competition irrelevant.* Boston: Harvard Business School Press.

Kotter, John P. 1996. *Leading change.* Boston: Harvard Business School Press.

Lehrer, Jonah. 2009. *How we decide.* New York: Houghton Mifflin Harcourt.

Lewin, Kurt. 1948. *Resolving social conflicts: Selected papers on group dynamics.* Ed. G. W. Lewin. New York: Harper & Row.

Ludema, James D., Diana Whitney, Bernard J. Mohr, and Thomas J. Griffin. 2003. *The Appreciative Inquiry Summit: A practitioner's guide for leading large-group change.* San Francisco: Berrett-Koehler.

Lukensmeyer, Carolyn J., and Wendy Jacobson. 2007. The 21st century town meeting: Engaging citizens in governance. In *The change handbook: The definitive resource on today's best methods for engaging whole systems*, Peggy Holman, Tom Devane, and Steven Cady, 393–398. San Francisco: Berrett-Koehler.

MacLeod, David, and Nita Clarke. 2009. *Engaging for success: Enhancing performance through employee engagement.* Department for Business Innovation and Skills. www.berr.gov.uk/files/file52215.pdf (accessed March 7, 2010).

McGregor, Douglas. 1960. *The human side of enterprise.* New York: McGraw-Hill.

McKinsey & Company. 2010. What successful transformations share: McKinsey Global Survey results. *McKinsey Quarterly*, March. http://www.mckinseyquarterly.com/Organization Change _Management/What_successful_transformations_share _McKinsey_Global_Survey_results_2550 (accessed March 17, 2010).

McMaster, Michael D. 1996. *The intelligence advantage: Organizing for complexity.* Boston: Butterworth-Heinemann.

Miller, Sherod, and Phyllis A. Miller. 1997. *Core communication: Skills and processes.* Evergreen, CO: Interpersonal Communications Programs.

Mintzberg, Henry. 2009. Rebuilding companies as communities. *Harvard Business Review*, July–August: 1–5 (reprint).

Owen, Harrison. 2008. *Open space technology: A user's guide.* San Francisco: Berrett-Koehler.

Pasmore, William A., and Gurudev S. Khalsa. 1993. The contributions of Eric Trist to the social engagement of social science. *Academy of Management Review* 18 (July): 546–569.

Plexus Institute. 2009. Positive deviance found to help fight drug-resistant infections. March 23, 2009. http://www.plexusinsti tute.org/news-events/show_news.cfm?id=1664 (accessed January 27, 2010).

Positive Deviance Initiative. How To/Getting Started with PD.
http://www.positivedeviance.org/about_pd/getting_started
.html (accessed November 18, 2009).

Putnam, Robert D. 1995. Bowling alone: America's declining social
capital. *Journal of Democracy* 6(1): 65–78.

Rehm, Robert. 2000. *People in charge: Creating self managing workplaces.* Gloucestershire, UK: Hawthorn Press.

Reina, Dennis S., and Michelle L. Reina. 2007. Building sustainable
trust. *OD Practitioner* 39(1): 36–41.

Rock, David. 2009. *Your brain at work: Strategies for overcoming
distraction, regaining focus, and working smarter all day long.*
New York: HarperCollins.

Rock, David, and Yiyuan Tang. 2009. Neuroscience of engagement. *NeuroLeadership Journal*, no. 2:15–22.

Senge, Peter M. 1990. *The fifth discipline: The art and practice of the
learning organization.* New York: Doubleday.

Senge, Peter M., Art Kleiner, Charlotte Roberts, Richard Ross,
George Roth, and Bryan Smith. 1999. *The dance of change: The
challenges to sustaining momentum in learning organizations.*
New York: Doubleday.

Simons, Tony. 2008. *The integrity dividend: Leading by the power of
your word.* San Francisco: Jossey-Bass.

Thackray, John. 2001. Feedback for real. *Gallup Management Journal*
(March 15). http://gmj.gallup.com/content/811/feedback-real
.aspx (accessed January 14, 2010).

Timberland. CSR: Community engagement. http://www.timber
land.com/corp/index.jsp?page=csr_civic_toolkit (accessed December 28, 2009).

Weisbord, Marvin R. 1987. *Productive workplaces: Organizing and
managing for dignity, meaning and community.* San Francisco:
Jossey-Bass.

Weisbord, Marvin R., and Sandra Janoff. 1995. *Future Search: An action guide to finding common ground in organizations and communities.* San Francisco: Berrett-Koehler.

Weisbord, Marvin R., and Sandra Janoff. 2000. *Future Search: An action guide to finding common ground in organizations and communities.* 2nd ed. San Francisco: Berrett-Koehler.

Wellins, Richard S., Paul Bernthal, and Mark Phelps. 2005. *Employee engagement: The key to realizing competitive advantage.* Monograph, Pittsburgh: Development Dimensions International.

West Monroe Partners. Press releases. http://www.westmonroe partners.com/West-Monroe-News/Press-Releases.aspx (accessed February 11, 2010).

ACKNOWLEDGMENTS

A t the end of every movie, the credits roll acknowledging everyone for his or her contribution; in the same way I want to acknowledge all those who gave their talents in support of *Terms of Engagement*. Let the credits roll.

THE STARS OF THE SHOW

To everyone I interviewed in preparation for this book, thanks for sharing your stories with me. Each in your own way influenced my thinking and helped me to formulate the ideas that are the basis of *Terms of Engagement*. Thank you to John Bader, Greg Balesteros, Paul Borawski, Sophia Christi, Bob Deahl, Linsey Dicks, Carol Gray, Tom Jorgenson, Susan Kinsey, Peter Koestenbaum, Jodi Krause, Louise Lang, Lenny Lind, Henri Lipmanowicz, Richard Marcello, Paulette McKissic, Susan Monaghan, Chris Moore, Gaetan Morency, David Rock, Darron Sandbergh, Shoji Shiba, Gary Short, Christ Trout, Leif Ulstrup, Tony Wickham, and Carla Zuniga.

I especially want to thank our clients for the privilege of working with you.

THE DIRECTOR

I have experienced firsthand the skill Steve Piersanti exhibits in dishing out penetrating criticism, always striving to make my work better. When he edits, he edits with one eye on what you are trying to say and one eye on what the reader wants to know. Not many people can do that. I've experienced Steve as a client as he puts into practice at Berrett-Koehler the ideas behind the books Berrett-Koehler publishes—where he holds fast to his belief that Berrett-Koehler has to work for all its stakeholders. I have experienced Steve as a smart, tough businessman as he led board of directors discussions. Editor, client, CEO—experiencing Steve in any one of these roles would be special. To experience Steve in all three roles is a treat.

THE COACH

Thanks so much to Nancy Breuer, owner of Facilio LLC and writing coach extraordinaire. Nancy coached, cajoled, and supported me into making this book into what it is today. Nancy and I had a running joke about how many corrections she could suggest in a draft chapter. The record was 180. Sorry I couldn't get to 200. If you find *Terms of Engagement* to the point and easy to read it's because I received great coaching from Nancy.

THE SUPPORTING CAST

To Peter Block, thanks for your insightful foreword and for being someone I can always turn to when I need help. The first edition of *Terms of Engagement* was forged in the crucible that was the School for Leading Change. Had you not invited

Emily and me to be faculty, *Terms of Engagement* would never had been written. To Peter Koestenbaum, you have given me a philosopher's worldview. You make me think. Sometimes my head hurts when we are done talking. But you always convey warmth, care, and humanness. To be around you is to be around a truly educated, compassionate human being. To Barbara Bunker, cofaculty in Columbia University's Principles and Practices in Organization Development program, you are a wonderful editor, colleague, and friend. I couldn't believe you were almost as excited as I was when I finished the manuscript. Thanks for your support and encouragement along the way. I'm a better teacher because of you. To Myron Rogers, thanks for being a thinking partner and for your special insights.

BEHIND THE SCENES

Special thanks to Rachel Singer for your diligence and attention to detail in preparing the manuscript while managing the affairs of the Axelrod Group. I don't know how you keep track of everything. I can't. Without you, the manuscript would have never been delivered on time and with such high quality. Thanks for being such a great partner.

Thanks to Sharon Goldinger, editor and owner of People-Speak, who was copyeditor. Your eye for the details is beyond 20/20, and your concern for the written word is here for everyone to see. You even made responding to your copyeditor's comments fun.

Thanks to Mary Ellen Gross, owner of Sizzle, for your support, excitement, and push as we work together to find the pitch perfect marketing for *Terms of Engagement*.

To all those who did critical reviews of the first edition and offered their insights for the second edition: thanks to Barbara

Bunker, Kathleen Flanigan, Jay Galbraith, Liz Guthridge, Jeff Kulick, Eric Linblad, Chris Trout, Leif Ulstrup, and Roopa Unnikrishnan. To Rosemarie Barbeau, Steve Treacy, and Nancy Voss, thanks for your support and friendship.

THE STAGE HANDS

Steve Piersanti has gathered a wonderful group of people who have helped bring this book to fruition. Special thanks to Dianne Platner for your skill and patience from cover design to final product. If you like the graphic summaries that precede each chapter, it was Dianne's idea to put them there. Rick Wilson, thanks for your excellent production assistance. Michael Crowley, Kristen Franz, and Katie Sheehan head up my sales and marketing team. I'm glad that you do.

THE ARTISTS

Good design takes something as mundane as the printed word and makes it pleasant for the eye to see. This is no small feat. The work of Bev Butterfield of Girl of the West Productions is here for all to see.

Joe Lafferty, owner of LifeTree, is a genius when it comes to turning my thoughts into images. The graphics at the beginning of each chapter are Joe's creation. Not only do they provide "coming attractions" for each chapter, they make my work come alive. Thank you for friendship and concern for my work.

THE PRODUCTION COMPANY

Berrett-Koehler is an extraordinary company. I have consulted to Berrett-Koehler, served on the board of directors, and authored two books with the company. In these three roles, I have learned firsthand what it means to be associated with impeccable integrity. Berrett-Koehler lives its values in good times and in bad times. When the people at Berrett-Koehler say they're dedicated to "Creating a World That Works for All," they mean it. They have demonstrated their values over and over again in the support I have received as an author, the hard work of the staff as I consulted with them, and the care and consideration given to decisions in the most difficult of times. I'm proud to say I'm a Berrett-Koehler author.

STAGE FAMILY

A special thanks to my Emily, to whom this book is dedicated. Thanks for reading draft after draft. Thanks for asking, "Is that what you really mean?" Thanks for being the voice of the reader in my head. But most of all after forty plus years of marriage, thanks for being Emily. To our son, David, thanks for your great coaching and assistance. To Kate, Dave's wife, thanks for your interest and support and for sharing your design expertise on the cover. To our daughter, Heather, thanks so much for your care and concern throughout this edition's birth. Simply asking, "Dad, how's it going?" meant a lot. To my grandsons, Zach (8) and Andy (6), thanks for climbing in my lap while I sat at the computer writing, reminding me by your presence that there is more to life than writing a book. I loved it when you saw the finished manuscript on my desk and said, "The cover is pretty. Grandpa, it's really big. How many pages are there?" To my mom, thanks for your interest and pride in what I do. You are the most courageous person I know. To my sister, Judy Siegal, thanks for your support, care, and concern. To my dad, I wish you were alive to read this book.

INDEX

ABOUT THE AXELROD GROUP

For more than twenty-nine years, the Axelrod Group has been at the forefront of organization change. The company's worldwide experience includes manufacturing, health care, banking, education, and government. The Axelrod Group's clients range from small not-for-profit organizations and community groups to Fortune 100 companies. Through these experiences, the Axelrod Group has developed a variety of proven processes and programs to increase employee engagement as well as customer service and productivity in almost any organization. They include the following:

- The New Change Management—described extensively in this book.

- Everyday Engagement—answers the question, We've done the engagement survey: now what?

- The Conference Model—helps you create strategic plans and redesign organizations and processes with the Axelrod Group's high-engagement approach.

- Collaborative Loops—builds your capacity to design high-engagement change processes in your organization.

- Executive Coaching—provides coaching as close as your phone.

- Consulting Skills—offers skills through Columbia University's Principles and Practices in Organization Development program, where Dick serves as a faculty member. Join him at Columbia or contact the company about bringing this program to your organization.
- Leadership with an Engagement Edge—provides training and coaching on the skills identified in this book.
- Sustainability—helps get everyone involved in this important work.

Beyond the book: Visit www.newtermsofengagement.com. Here you will find additional cases, articles, and PowerPoint presentations you can use.

Coming attractions: An app to improve your engagement skills using the key points from *Terms of Engagement* and a wealth of other resources.

Our Web sites: www.axelrodgroup.com, www.everydayengagement.com, www.axelrodcommunity.com

Contact us: info@axelrodgroup.com, **847-251-7361**.

ABOUT THE AUTHOR

Brad Baskin Photography

Dick Axelrod and his wife, Emily, co-founded the Axelrod Group, Inc., a consulting firm that pioneered the use of employee involvement to effect large-scale organizational change. He now brings more than thirty-five years of consulting and teaching experience to this work, with clients including Boeing, Coca-Cola, Harley-Davidson, Hewlett-Packard, and the National Health Service (UK). Dick is a faculty member in Columbia University's Principles and Practices in Organization Development program and the University of Chicago's Leadership Arts program. He serves on the Board of Directors of Berrett-Koehler Publishers. Dick authored *Terms of Engagement: Changing the Way We Change Organizations* and coauthored *You Don't Have to Do It Alone: How to Involve Others to Get Things Done*, which the *New York Times* called "the best of the current crop of books on this subject."

Before forming the Axelrod Group, Dick was an organization development manager for General Foods, which was the first company in America to use self-directed work teams (a strategy whose philosophy made a great impact on the young manager). He also served in the U.S. Army in Korea as a micro-wave radio officer.

Dick is a contributor to numerous books, including *The Change Handbook*, *The Flawless Consulting Fieldbook and Companion*, and *The Handbook of Large Group Methods*. His articles have appeared in *Harvard Management Update*, *Fast Company*, the *Society for Organizational Learning Journal*, and *Healthcare Quarterly*, to name a few.

Dick and Emily have been married for more than forty years. They live outside of Chicago in Wilmette, Illinois. They have three adult children, Heather and David and his wife, Kate, and two grandchildren, Zachary and Andrew, who are the joys of their lives. Dick is a long-suffering Chicago Cubs fan.

Also by Richard H. Axelrod, with Emily M. Axelrod,
Julie Beedon, and Robert W. Jacobs

You Don't Have to Do It Alone
How to Involve Others to Get Things Done

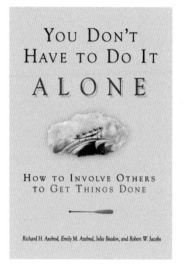

We all need to involve others to accomplish tasks and achieve our goals, but
all too often involving others seems like more trouble than it's worth. This
book is the Swiss Army knife of involvement, offering a set of tools that can
be used in any setting to get you the help you need. The authors lay out a
simple, straightforward plan that begins with five key questions. The answers
to these questions serve as a guide to finding the right people and keeping
them energized, enthusiastic, and committed until the work is completed.

*"The best of the current crop of books on this topic...gives you a complete
blueprint for involving others."*
   —**Paul B. Brown, *New York Times***

"This book is an excellent resource!"
   —**Ken Blanchard, author of *The One Minute Manager***

Paperback, 120 pages, ISBN 978-1-57675-278-4
PDF ebook, ISBN 978-1-57675-879-3

BK Berrett–Koehler Publishers, Inc.
   www.bkconnection.com   **800.929.2929**

Berrett–Koehler
Publishers

Berrett-Koehler is an independent publisher dedicated to an ambitious mission: *Creating a World That Works for All.*

We believe that to truly create a better world, action is needed at all levels—individual, organizational, and societal. At the individual level, our publications help people align their lives with their values and with their aspirations for a better world. At the organizational level, our publications promote progressive leadership and management practices, socially responsible approaches to business, and humane and effective organizations. At the societal level, our publications advance social and economic justice, shared prosperity, sustainability, and new solutions to national and global issues.

A major theme of our publications is "Opening Up New Space." Berrett-Koehler titles challenge conventional thinking, introduce new ideas, and foster positive change. Their common quest is changing the underlying beliefs, mindsets, institutions, and structures that keep generating the same cycles of problems, no matter who our leaders are or what improvement programs we adopt.

We strive to practice what we preach—to operate our publishing company in line with the ideas in our books. At the core of our approach is stewardship, which we define as a deep sense of responsibility to administer the company for the benefit of all of our "stakeholder" groups: authors, customers, employees, investors, service providers, and the communities and environment around us.

We are grateful to the thousands of readers, authors, and other friends of the company who consider themselves to be part of the "BK Community." We hope that you, too, will join us in our mission.

A BK Business Book

This book is part of our BK Business series. BK Business titles pioneer new and progressive leadership and management practices in all types of public, private, and nonprofit organizations. They promote socially responsible approaches to business, innovative organizational change methods, and more humane and effective organizations.

Berrett–Koehler
Publishers

A community dedicated to creating
a world that works for all

Visit Our Website: www.bkconnection.com

Read book excerpts, see author videos and Internet movies, read our authors'
blogs, join discussion groups, download book apps, find out about the BK
Affiliate Network, browse subject-area libraries of books, get special discounts, and more!

Subscribe to Our Free E-Newsletter, the *BK Communiqué*

Be the first to hear about new publications, special discount offers, exclu-
sive articles, news about bestsellers, and more! Get on the list for our free
e-newsletter by going to **www.bkconnection.com**.

Get Quantity Discounts

Berrett-Koehler books are available at quantity discounts for orders of ten or
more copies. Please call us toll-free at (800) 929-2929 or email us at bkp
.orders@aidcvt.com.

Join the BK Community

BKcommunity.com is a virtual meeting place where people from around the
world can engage with kindred spirits to create a world that works for all.
BKcommunity.com members may create their own profiles, blog, start and
participate in forums and discussion groups, post photos and videos, answer
surveys, announce and register for upcoming events, and chat with others
online in real time. Please join the conversation!

© **Mixed Sources**
Product group from well-managed
forests, controlled sources and
recycled wood or fiber
www.fsc.org Cert no. SW-COC-003925
FSC © 1996 Forest Stewardship Council